The Route taken
on his journey to Japan

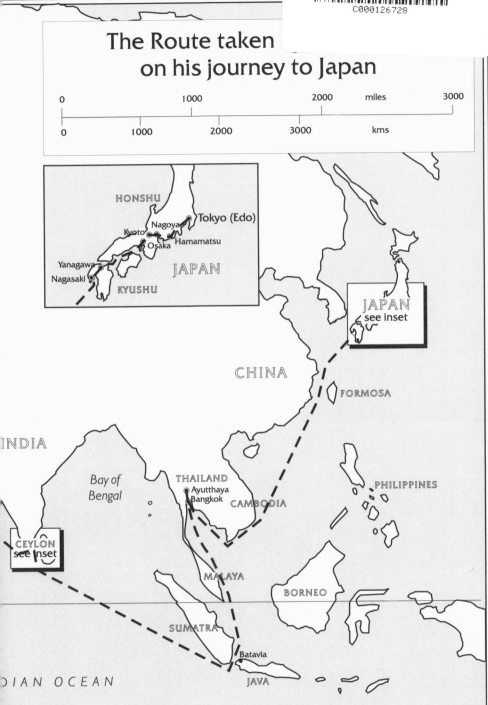

Engelbert Kaempfer

Engelbert Kaempfer
1651-1716

A biography

Detlef Haberland
Translated by Peter Hogg

The British Library
1996

© 1996 Detlef Haberland
© 1996 English translation Peter Hogg
First published 1996
by The British Library
Great Russell Street
London WC1B 3DG

Photographic Acknowledgements
All illustrations are reproduced by permission of The British Library Board,
with the exception of the following: Lippische Landesbibliothek, Detmold,
figs.1, 10, 11, 15, 16, 20, 33, 54; Lippisches Landesmuseum, Detmold, fig.51;
Prentenkabinet der Rijksuniversiteit, Leiden, fig.50; The Trustees of the
British Museum, fig.53.

Cataloguing in Publication Data is available from
The British Library

ISBN 0 7123 4503 5

Designed by John Trevitt
Typeset in Monotype Ehrhardt
by Nene Phototypesetters, Northampton
Printed in England by St Edmundsbury Press, Bury St Edmunds

Contents

Foreword and acknowledgements

Engelbert Kaempfer's life now seems remote from us in two respects: the period during which he lived has become alien and in part unintelligible to us, and the exotic cultures of the countries through which he travelled no longer exist in the form in which Kaempfer experienced them. However, by discovering the circumstances and activities of exceptional individuals from that period, even if they did not play a significant public role, much can be learnt about the history, not only of our own but also of the other cultures.

Kaempfer left an enormous amount of manuscripts, drawings and objects, which the great collector Sir Hans Sloane acquired at the beginning of the eighteenth century and made available to a scholarly public by incorporating them in his collection, which was to form the basis of the British Museum. The most extensive literary remains of a German traveller of the seventeenth century were thus preserved and are today available for research.

Kaempfer has consequently come to be directly associated with the history of ideas in England, as his work forms a not insignificant part of the history of the British Museum, the British Library, the Natural History Museum and the Museum of Mankind and is therefore, at a more general level, closely linked to the history of collecting in England during the eighteenth century.

The author owes the fact that this biography can be presented to English-speaking readers to a series of fortunate circumstances, but above all to the friendly professional encouragement that he received in many quarters. The following in particular deserve to be mentioned. Yu-Ying Brown (Head of the Japanese Section, Oriental and India Office Collections, British Library) suggested the inclusion of a translation of the biography, which was originally published in German, in the publications programme of the British Library. David Way (of the Publishing Office, British Library) was at all stages of the planning and production of the book a shrewd and always good-humoured editor. The clear and workmanlike style of the present version of the book is primarily due to the excellent translator, Peter Hogg (of the Scandinavian Section, British

Library), who diligently drew attention to difficulties until all were resolved.

Finally, the author is indebted to the Chief Executive of the British Library, Dr Brian Lang, for his courtesy and helpfulness with regard to Kaempfer generally and this biography in particular.

During every research visit to London the staff of the Department of Manuscripts Students' Room in the British Library have not only been available for assistance but have provided active help; Michael Boggan and Annie Gilbert, who organised the reproduction of the illustrations, deserve special mention.

Only the financial support provided for the translation by Inter Nationes in Bonn made it possible to plan the English edition; Dr Angelika Uerling-Folle, in particular, has involved herself in the project in a committed and co-operative spirit and has helped to bring it to realisation.

For information, stimulus, support and criticism the author is grateful to the following friends and colleagues: Prof. Hanno Beck (Bonn), Winrich C.-W. Clasen (Rheinbach), Dr Albertine Gaur (London), Dr Detlev Hellfaier (Lippische Landesbibliothek, Detmold), Johannes Hettling (Lemgo), Prof. Brigitte Hoppe (Munich), Dr Peter Kapitza (Munich), Prof. Josef Kreiner (Tokyo), Dr Peter Krüger (Berlin), Dr Dieter Merzbacher (Herzog August Bibliothek, Wolfenbüttel), Prof. Wolfgang Michel (Fukuoka), Prof. Peter Pantzer (Bonn), Beatrice Rauschenbach M.A. (Munich), Dr Michael Schippan (Berlin), Herbert Stöwer (Engelbert-Kämpfer-Gesellschaft, Detmold), Dr Paul van de Velde (Leiden), Prof. Josef Wiesehöfer (Kiel), Dr Elke K. Werger-Klein (Utrecht) and Dr Gisela Wilbertz (Stadtarchiv, Lemgo). Last but not least I owe thanks to my wife for her unflagging sympathy and active interest during the preparation of this edition.

DETLEF HABERLAND

Bonn/London, October 1996

1. *Introduction*

Thirty-six years have passed since the appearance in 1960 of the second edition of Karl Meier-Lemgo's biography of Engelbert Kaempfer, written as a 'book for the people' with the aim of making Kaempfer familiar to a wider audience. That biography has long been out of print. During the intervening years a number of interesting and valuable special studies have been published, while the international symposia held in Lemgo and Tokyo in 1990 produced many stimulating ideas. However, the products of research on individual topics are no substitute for a general account based on scholarly principles.

Apart from that, Kaempfer's varied and complex life story reads like a novel and is worth telling for that reason alone. Kaempfer, who was a qualified physician and spoke several languages, was acutely observant and became during his career a master draughtsman. In addition, he rapidly acquainted himself with the most recondite fields of study, in which he wrote with accuracy and in some cases as a pioneer. His topics ranged from the archaeology of Persia to Japanese history and from cartography to botany and medicine.

This wide variety, of course, made it difficult for posterity to gain an overview of his – largely unpublished – work. Nevertheless, those of Kaempfer's writings that did become known belong to the essential core of seventeenth-century literature on travel and cultural history. Moreover, he always occupied a distinguished place in the history of European research on Japan.

After more than thirty years of Kaempfer studies on an international scale one thing has become clearer than ever, however – it is no longer enough to try to judge Kaempfer on the basis of the extensively revised editions of his work produced single-handedly by Meier-Lemgo. It has become indispensable to return to the source – and that means to the British Library, where the traveller's unpublished papers, acquired in 1723 and 1725 by Sir Hans Sloane, are preserved.

It is the aim of every biography to bring alive before the mind's eye of the reader the personality of its subject and to describe the person's actions and their causes. For various reasons the realisation of that aim meets with certain difficulties in the case of the present work. Kaempfer's writings have not yet by any means been fully and satisfactorily edited, while sources of a personal nature are relatively scarce and can often be transcribed only with great difficulty owing to the poor state of preservation of some of them. Finally, for the above reasons as well as the distance in time, the motives for many individual acts as well as aspects of the wider context are now inaccessible to us. Unfortunately, too, there is as yet no known portrait of Kaempfer which might have conveyed an impression of him as a human being. That circumstance does have the advantage, however, of compelling us to reassesss and reinterpret every scrap of information in attempting to delineate his personality.

Thus the present work should appeal to two kinds of readers rather than to one. It addresses itself equally to those who are concerned, either actually or potentially, with Kaempfer himself and to those who are interested in the history of travel, science and culture. While the references and notes may be a less essential feature for the former, they will, I hope, provide guidance and suggestions for the latter. Their justification lies not least in the fact that the conditions for research have changed entirely since the time of Meier-Lemgo's biography. His image of Kaempfer, sketched with great verve, has become problematic in the light of more recent research and of an historical awareness that has been utterly transformed compared with what it was in 1937 and 1960. A new presentation in terms of biography and the history of travel can no longer serve the purpose of conveying an idealistically heightened picture. It must reveal everything that appears possible and conceivable within the historical context, but also that which is problematic, and thus attempt to get closer to the reality, exceedingly strange though it may be.

The situation outlined above with regard to the sources makes it impossible to provide conclusive answers to every question. Instead of presenting a speculatively rounded account of Kaempfer and his aims, the places where gaps in the record are apparent will be identified as such. In these areas future research on Kaempfer will still have many problems to resolve.

2. *Family, youth and schooldays*

Engelbert Kaempfer's family is extensively documented.[1] His paternal ancestors have been traced as far back as the first third of the sixteenth century as stewards of a family called Wendt in Wiedenbrück whose own roots were in Lemgo. Margareta Flörcke, the wife of Jodokus Kemper, Engelbert's grandfather, also came from an old Lemgo family. That may explain why Engelbert's father looked to Lemgo for a career.

The latter, Johannes Kemper, was born on 10 July 1610 as the son of Jodokus Kemper in Wiedenbrück. After attending the municipal primary school there, then the famous grammar school in Soest and, from 1632, the grammar school in Lemgo, he studied in Rostock and Rinteln. At the early age of 27 he became choirmaster and lector at the Latin school in Lemgo but then spent another two years in Rostock, where he took a master's degree. Having become curate of St Nicholas' Church in Lemgo in 1642, he was promoted to vicar, or *pastor primarius*, there in 1644.

Johannes Kemper was married for the first time in 1644 to Christine Drepper, the daughter of his predecessor in office. This marriage produced a daughter, who died young, and three sons: Joachim (1646-1706), Engelbert (1651-1716) and Johann (†1703). After the death of his first wife, around 1654, Johannes married again, this time Adelheid Pöppelmann (1637-1721), the sister of the wife of Andreas Koch, the curate at St Nicholas. She bore him five children: Andreas (1658-1743), Johann Heinrich (†1717), Johann Daniel (†1709), Maria Magdalena (1669-1711) and Anna Catharina (1673-1749). Kemper himself died on 31 August 1682.

In describing the family network, it is evident that there was a change of name among the Kempers. All his life Engelbert's father, like his ancestors, signed himself 'Kemper', a name presumably derived from the Westphalian word *Kamp*.[2] Engelbert himself entered his name in the register of the grammar school in Lemgo as 'Engelbertus Kemper, Lemgovia-Westphalus'.[3]

During the course of his life he signs his name in different ways, alternating between the variants 'Kemper' and 'Kempfer'.[4] On the title-page of the *Exercitatio politica*, which appeared in 1673, the name is already

3

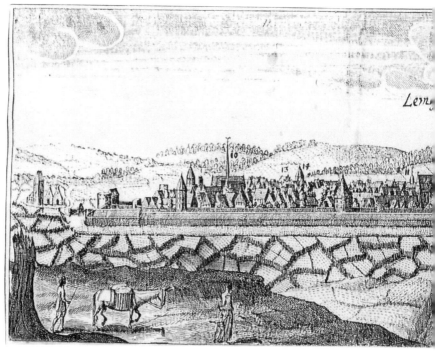

1. Lemgo, around 1650. Engraving by Elias von Lennep, 1663.

given as 'Kaempfer' (with a superscript e over the a). Although the form 'Kempfer' reappears on the title-page of the dissertation published in 1694, Kaempfer again uses the form 'Kaempfer' in his *Amoenitates exoticae* in 1712. Finally, he signs his will[5] as 'Kämpffer'. The form 'Kaempfer' adopted in recent years, for example in the *Festschrift* for the 330th anniversary of his birth, is therefore a reasonable compromise and preferable to all other variants of the name.

This mutation of names is by no means the result of caprice, whether from thoughtlessness or a lack of tradition, but rather evidence of a social transformation that took place during and, even more frequently, after the Thirty Years' War.[6] In this regard the Kemper family, so to speak, exemplifies those who rose from the class of peasants and craftsmen into that of the educated middle class. The preferred form 'Kaempfer' also expresses a baroque characteristic – the play on symbolic and metaphorical etymologies of names which were not, of course, scientifically exact. The giving of names within the literary societies that set the tone for the

educated classes is part of the same trend. Analogous to Kaempfer's case is that of Martin Opitz, for instance, who as poet laureate was referred to as 'the Crowned'. An expression of that approach is the prize poem of Engelbert's brother Joachim, which includes the following lines:

> By the mere sense of your name you are held in duty towards it;
> Both things, oh Kämpfer, are yours, *nomen et omen habes.*
> If as a youth the arena you enter, the prize that awaits you,
> When the contest is over, is to step out as a man.[7]

Kaempfer's name was thus interpreted as signifying a struggle for existence, in the sense of a spiritual and intellectual contest for knowledge, faith and learning. And that is also how the Rev. Haccius understood it when he said at Engelbert's graveside, referring to the deceased: 'On the roads of this temporal life we face many struggles. In the actual physical sense that is a matter of common knowledge.'[8]

Engelbert was born in Lemgo on 16 September 1651, three years after the end of the Thirty Years' War. Although there was no longer

protracted warfare in the county of Lemgo, the situation was still dominated by the troops that remained in the territory and could only slowly
be persuaded to withdraw. Moreover, hunger, misery and poverty pre-
vailed everywhere, so that not only in Lemgo generally but even in the
vicarage itself life must have been conducted at a fairly modest level.[9]

Despite all the privations, the Rev. Kemper made sure that his sons had
a good education which, as in his own case, would enable them to rise in
the social and economic scale.[10] He himself set them a good example in
this regard through his varied interests and eagerness to improve his
mind, which is clearly reflected in his library.[11] Hence Engelbert was sent
to the grammar school in his native town from 1665 onward. Here he
began by learning reading, writing and arithmetic and also acquired a
grounding in the natural sciences, besides the rudiments of the classical
languages.[12]

It is hardly likely that Engelbert's desire to see foreign lands had already
become so focussed during his schooldays that he contemplated a particular professional career abroad. There is no surviving evidence – as we
know nothing at all about his personal experiences during his childhood
and youth – that could justify the notion that he had already adopted such
a goal at an early age. It is probably the statement in the *Nachricht von dem
Lebens-Lauff des wohlsel. Herrn D. Kaempfers* – 'As the now deceased Doctor had since his youth felt a particular eagerness to see foreign places and
to complete his studies elsewhere, he at first, with his father's consent,
went from here to Hameln [...]'[13] – that first gave rise to this idea, which
has been uncritically accepted even in recent publications. It is enough to
cite the statement by Hoppe, who is convinced 'that he had at an early
stage conceived a plan for world-wide [!] journeys of exploration and
prepared himself systematically to enter the service of one of the powers
that were involved in international trade relations or were endeavouring
to establish them'.[14]

It is no longer possible, of course, to ascertain whether Haccius already
derived the idea retrospectively from Kaempfer's life. Once the notion
had been transmitted in that form during the eighteenth and nineteenth
centuries – with Dohm, a man of the Enlightenment, making his own
special contribution – it was above all Meier-Lemgo who propagated it,
authoritatively and constantly restated. ('To become an explorer: that was
clearly from the start his fixed and settled goal.'[15]) Even his father's
library can only provide qualified evidence as, due to the sale of the books,
it is now impossible to determine which of them were actually there

before Engelbert's departure. The copy of Olearius' *Moskowitischer und persianischer Reise* (1654) that belonged to the Rev. Kemper has indeed survived, and other works of travel are also known to have been in his library – but does that fact really suffice to prove the 'particular eagerness' of which Haccius speaks? Nor is there any proof of the assumption that he was actually 'driven out' by the 'poisoned' atmosphere in the town caused by the witchcraft trials.[16]

On the other hand, it is of course inconceivable that he knew nothing about the witch-hunts, in view of the fact that his own father, as pastor, had an official duty to offer spiritual counsel to the victims and that the year 1666, when he was still at school in Lemgo, saw a higher number of trials (34) than any other until 1681.[17] As early as 1665 his father's brother-in-law, the pastor Andreas Koch, had been indicted and executed.

The reason why he changed schools and places of residence was rather the customary system of studying at several schools (or universities), so that pupils and students, like craftsmen, moved from place to place and from one professor to another.[18]

In addition, his father's position in the town was obviously so strong that, despite his openly expressed criticism of the extremely murky events (which were common knowledge), he could not be denounced and prosecuted.[19] All speculation regarding the wishes and desires of the young Engelbert Kaempfer should therefore be suspended until relevant evidence is discovered.[20] What is certain, however, is that he absorbed the solid outlook and diligence of a Westphalian paterfamilias in his childhood home, as well as the uprightness and neighbourliness of a Lutheran pastor, qualities that he retained throughout his life: 'Thus the house of the blessed Doctor was never closed to all those who were needy, nor to the poor and the wretched, whether they were strangers or local people, but stood open to serve almost everyone, while his beneficence was unreserved.'[21] The Rev. Kemper's life shows clearly that in his educational and social ambitions he operated wholly within the framework of absolutist moral concepts.[22]

The only certain assumption one can make is that Engelbert must have tried to acquire as much knowledge as possible so that (like his father) he would later be able to attain a corresponding position in society. His striving for respectability is also underlined by the fact that he chose the local ruler and his wife as godparents for his first and third child.

3. *The years of study*

After spending his first two years of schooling in Lemgo, Engelbert moved to the school in Hameln in 1667. Here he lived with relatives of his, Hermann Prott and his family.[1] The cost of his education away from home was therefore comparatively low. It was probably at this time that he made a journey to Holland, but whom he visited and where he went is unknown.[2] Nor is there any evidence that on this occasion he was deliberately looking around there for employment or for a place in which to study.[3] One can only speculate about Kaempfer's reasons for deciding not to study in the Netherlands – there is no documentary evidence for his decision.

In 1668 he moved from Hameln to Lüneburg, where he attended the local grammar school and 'made excellent progress *in philologicis, historicis & geographicis*'[4] under Professor Kettenbeil – in other words, he studied these subjects diligently. It is interesting that Haccius finds it worth emphasising that Kaempfer achieved a certain competence both in singing and in playing an instrument.[5] He developed a natural talent into a skill that was valued in baroque society.[6] While at first it is simply the breadth of his interests that is remarkable, he was later to demonstrate his ability to apply the knowledge that he had acquired. For example, in his treatise on the date-palm he also makes a thorough investigation of the cultural activities that took place during the period of the date-harvest, including a detailed account of the music that was played in the evenings for relaxation.[7]

From Lüneburg he moved on to Mecklenburg, Holstein and Hamburg[8] and from there to Lübeck, whose grammar school was renowned.[9] Here, as in Lüneburg, he studied classical languages as well as philosophy under Professor Hermann Nottelmann (1626-74).[10] In 1672 he went on to Danzig, where he pursued his studies at the Athenaeum. His choice of Danzig as a place to study was no more fortuitous than his previous choices. Its grammar school, founded in 1558 in the course of the Reformation, had gained a 'considerable reputation[11] through the work of the eminent Reformed academic philosopher Bartholomäus Keckermann (1571-1608)[12] as well as the Lutherans Johannes Botsack (1600-74) from

8

ASPIRANTE SANCTA TRIADE!
EXERCITATIO POLITICA
DE
MAJESTATIS
DIVISIONE
IN
REALEM ET PERSONALEM,
Quam
PRÆSIDE
Excellentisfimo juxta ac Clarisfimo
V I R O,
DN. M. GEORGIO Neufeld/
Philof. Pract. Metaph. Logicæq; Prof. Ord.
& Bibliothec.
Promotore, Fautore ac Præceptore fuo
omni ætate Obfervando,
In Celeberr. Gedanenfium Athenæi
Auditorio Maximo
Valedictionis loco
Publicè ventilandam proponit
ENGELBERTUS Kämpffer/
Lemgoviâ Weftphalus.
A. C. M. DC. LXXIII. d. 8. Junii h. mat.
DANTISCI, Imprimebat DAVID-FRIDERICUS RHETIUS.

2. *Exercitatio politica*, title-page of Kaempfer's first publication. With essays like this grammar-school pupils proved their aptitude for higher education.

Herford and Abraham Calov (1612-84) from Mohrungen, who were at various times headmasters of the school. Kaempfer completed his studies on 8 June 1673 with the obligatory disputation under Professor Georg Neufeld (1625-73).[13]

By means of such a debate and an accompanying written dissertation a pupil proved his suitability for academic studies. It could not be expected, therefore, that the submitted essay would be a mature work. Its purpose was rather to show that he had mastered Latin, the methods of source analysis and citation and the compilation of a short treatise.[14] In his essay *Exercitatio politica de majestatis divisione in realem et personalem [...]* Kaempfer dealt with a thoroughly topical theme – the question of the division of powers within the state – a central problem that, with absolutism at the height of its development, had been the subject of study by a number of constitutional lawyers and was thus well suited to a work of this kind.[15] Kaempfer proceeds scrupulously. After explaining the etymology of the concept of 'majesty', he defines both that notion and the idea of divisibility (*divisibilitas*). Having enumerated the arguments both for and against the divisibility of majesty, he concludes that earthly majesty derives from the grace of God and stands above the law.[16] By concluding, from the single sentence that the king exists 'due to the necessity of devoting himself and his life to the welfare of the people',[17] that one can attribute to the young Kaempfer an attitude corresponding more or less to 'enlightened absolutism',[18] Meier-Lemgo fails to appreciate the historical logic in the evolution of the theory of constitutional law. On the contrary, in expressing this opinion, Kaempfer still remains entirely in the tradition of Christian legitimisation of monarchy which lasted into the eighteenth century. The definition of the monarch as a 'servant of God' who should act for the good of his subjects (which in practice did not preclude baroque displays of pomp!) became effectively true only around the middle of the eighteenth century when his office, founded on natural law, became one of serving the reason of state.[19] All in all, Kaempfer's approach is rather immature, especially as the exposition visibly falters towards the end, and it does not yet foreshadow the superb scholar of later years.[20] In this work he defends absolutism against the theory of natural law and thus aligns himself with one of the two main ideological currents of his time.[21]

Although the essay is far from original, it must have seemed good enough to Kaempfer's teachers for them to encourage him to have it printed. There is a reason for that, which is evident as soon as one opens the work, namely that Kaempfer has developed his theme with precision and strict adherence to the scholastic scheme of argumentation. Whether he paid for the printing himself or his father or the school financed it, we do not know.

During the next few years he studied at various places in the kingdom of Poland. This period can best be understood with the help of the album amicorum (*Stammbuch*) that he kept from 1674 to 1694.[22] In addition, the early biographical accounts – above all that of Haccius, but also those by Scheuchzer, Niceron, Jöcher and later Dohm – should not be undervalued as sources of information. Not only does their wording incorporate much evidence derived from contemporaries but, owing to their proximity in time and outlook, they frequently produced a characterisation that gets closer to the truth than many later statements.[23]

From Danzig, then an autonomous Hanseatic city under Polish protective sovereignty, Kaempfer travelled by way of Torun to Cracow. The fact is, however, that between the date of the disputation in Danzig on 8 June 1673 and the first entry in the album there lies a whole year for which we have no information. He appears to have spent that year in Torun, a city in no way inferior to Danzig – for 'a certain time', as Dohm writes.[24] It is not known whether he was studying or earning money during that period.

The next stage was Piotrkow, where the president of the crown tribunal, Johann Lukoski, wrote a friendly entry in Kaempfer's album.[25] These lines are especially informative. He had become personally acquainted with Lukoski and had been a guest in his house, 'in the presence of many of my friends', as the latter remarked.[26] When Lukoski writes that Kaempfer 'travelled through Piotrkow on the way to distant nations'[27] it may therefore be interpreted as a direct reflection of something Kaempfer himself said in conversation regarding a more remote destination. Although the passage is unfortunately not a direct quotation, it does represent – at the start of his undergraduate years – the very first occasion when one can say that Kaempfer was thinking of going abroad. It is obviously impossible to decide on the basis of the entry whether that meant 'merely' Sweden or the Orient.

The next place to attract him for further studies was Cracow. Even in Kaempfer's day the university of the old capital of Poland was still an important centre of research and teaching, despite the persisting influence of scholasticism in the seventeenth century and the reluctant acceptance of humanist ideas. Medicine expanded rapidly here from 1604 onward, the number of professorships rising from six to seventeen. Philology, history and Greek were highly developed along humanist lines and were taught, like mathematics and astronomy, at an advanced level.[28] Here Kaempfer studied primarily medicine and philosophy until 1676. From the entries written by the professors at the end of his time at the university it is clear[29] that, apart from his basic subjects, he also improved himself 'in the knowledge of foreign languages, nations and countries', as Haccius expressed it.[30] After four terms Kaempfer completed his studies in Cracow. It must remain an open question whether he gained the title of *magister artium*, but that is unlikely, as he never used it himself and is not referred to as such in any surviving letter.[31]

We can follow his progress from Cracow through Warsaw (29 May 1676),[32] Torun (6 June), Danzig (13-17 June) and Elbing (23 June) to Königsberg. Here another gap appears in his biography; we do not know what he did during the nine months between the last entry made in Elbing (23 June 1676) and his registering at the university in Königsberg the following year. As there is no evidence that he attended any other university, it is possible that – as he may have done during 1673/74 – he took some lowly position (perhaps as a private tutor, as in Königsberg?) in order to earn his living.

In that way, as he had already done in Torun and Cracow, he continually met representatives of the administration and scholarship, noblemen and, of course, former teachers, whose entries in his album refer to him in a series of flattering eulogies: they speak of Kaempfer as a very diligent student (*diligentissimo auditori*), highly educated (*literatissimo*), high-minded (*generoso*) and most learned (*doctissimo*), as well as an exceptionally avid reader (*eximio philothecario*). All these formulations indicate that Kaempfer was held in uniformly high regard. Even if one makes allowance for the elevated tone and panegyric purpose of the entries, we can fully accept Dohm's assessment as a characterisation of him: 'That Kaempfer not only educated himself in his study but also in the world and society I infer from the fact that he was able to make the acquaintance here in Cracow of Baron Alexander Lubomirski and of the privy councillor and special envoy of the elector of Brandenburg to the Polish Diet, von Hoverbeck. If men of such high standing think it worth giving their attention to a young man and receiving him in their homes, then this certainly conveys a very positive view of the young scholar as well as of the perspicacity of the great men, when their earlier opinion is subsequently confirmed by that of the general public.'[33]

From 13 March 1677 Kaempfer can be traced in Königsberg, where he enrolled himself at the Albertus University as a law student,[34] though he gave priority to medicine, as is shown by the number of entries in his album written by his teachers.[35] However, the assumption that he studied the still new-fangled subject of natural history[36] is not confirmed by the album and can be traced only as far back as Dohm. Earlier sources, such as Haccius, do not mention it.[37] Nevertheless, Kaempfer's many-sided interests in the field of natural sciences – for which he must have acquired much of his skill and knowledge during his years as a student – undoubtedly point to corresponding studies at one or other of the universities, even if the evidence for it is lacking. The actual choice of subjects did not have to coincide with the registration.

Just as Kaempfer's earlier choice of schools in Lübeck, Danzig and Torun and of the university in Cracow were in no way determined simply by a love of travelling, it is also easy to see a connection between his attendance at the university in Königsberg and his personal interests. That city, which had been linked in a union with Brandenburg since 1618, was still a flourishing community despite many political and economic difficulties.[38] Despite the constantly recurring religious conflicts, the university was a Protestant foundation. Although it could hardly be described as one of the most progressive ones during that period, it was a centre of attraction for natural scientists due to its rich endowments, above all the Wallenrodt library, Panzer's pharmacy and the important botanical garden.[39] Its cultural life was also quite highly developed, owing to the Königsberg circle of poets and the historical and still continuing influence of the latter.[40] It is thus understandable why Kaempfer chose to study here.

Another factor also inevitably comes to mind when one thinks of Königsberg in the seventeenth century. Here, as in Torun, the Swedish influence was incalculable. In three wars (1626-9, 1655-60 and 1672-9) the Swedes had demonstrated their ambition to exercise power in north-eastern Europe. Although they never held power directly for very long, they did emerge as the one Baltic state with a claim to hegemony. The undisguised Swedish presence certainly made Kaempfer aware of the political and therefore also of the economic power of Charles XI. Finally, the connections of Lemgo with the Baltic region and Sweden through long-distance trade had been cultivated since the Middle Ages.[41] His resolve to go to Sweden after completing his studies is likely, if not to have originated here, then at least to have been reinforced. The example of Samuel Pufendorf, who had attained the position of Swedish court historiographer and secretary of state, was no doubt known to him.

The decision of Engelbert's stepbrother Andreas to go to Sweden may not have been entirely voluntary, if one is to believe Andreas's autobiography, which is the only source for his decision.[42] On the whole, however, it must have been the latter's professional success, among other factors, that caused Engelbert to follow him to Sweden.

The reason why he did not complete his studies at this stage by obtaining a doctorate in medicine can, of course, only be conjectured. Perhaps his age made him feel the need to look for permanent employment, or else he lacked the means to pay for the conferment ceremony and the printing of the dissertation.[43] Be that as it may, Kaempfer did not allow even the lack of financial resources to deter him from further studies. Perhaps his father's entry in his album (see below) should also be seen in that light.

He never received a large monthly allowance from home, for it is recorded that he taught the nephews of the abbess of Tettau in Königsberg.[44] However, to accept a position as private tutor was nothing unusual at that time and had the added advantage of offering an education in 'the world and society'.[45]

Only once did Kaempfer go on 'home leave' to see his father in Lieme, where he had retired. He left Königsberg, probably in August 1680, and travelled by way of Lübeck to Westphalia.[46] This was his last reunion with his father, who died in 1682. It is consistent with his upright Protestant outlook and perhaps also with his concern for Engelbert, that Johannes Kemper wrote in his son's album: 'Learn as if you would live forever, live as if you would die today.' And: 'Strive rather for a good conscience than for a good reputation. For one's reputation may often be deceptive, but never one's conscience.'[47]

Engelbert left Lieme with his brother Andreas on 25 October; he had thus been at home for over a month. They travelled by way of Verden an der Aller, Bremen and Hamburg to Lübeck,[48] where their ways parted. Andreas wanted to go straight on to Stockholm, and Engelbert returned to the University in Königsberg. He studied there for almost another year and travelled via Danzig to Sweden in August 1681.[49]

4. *From Sweden to Persia*

In Uppsala and Stockholm

In Sweden Kaempfer made his way to Uppsala, the leading Scandinavian university, where the universal scholar Olof Rudbeck (1630-1702)[1] provided a focus of academic attraction. Dohm's assumption 'that the acquaintance with this scholar had an influence on Kaempfer's studies'[2] is undoubtedly correct. Even in Sweden the impact of modern scientific theories and methods was felt: 'in the sixties of the seventeenth century the ideas of Descartes gained ground among the natural scientists, i.e. in the medical faculty, where Olof Rudbeck and his colleague Hoffwenius, a distinguished and steadfast man, defended the new perception of nature.'[3] Here, if not already in Königsberg, Kaempfer's talent for precise observation of his surroundings and accurate recording of what he saw became thoroughly disciplined.[4]

By this time at the latest he can no longer have been thinking only of extending his knowledge. He was now thirty years old and still without a professional and social position, even if he did gain the support of important men in Sweden, as he had already done in the Empire.[5] At this point Dohm's conclusion regarding the decisive change in Kaempfer's life is no doubt apt: 'Kaempfer distinguished himself so much at the university by his talents and knowledge that these also won him patrons and friends in Stockholm, and that among the most eminent and worthy men in the kingdom. [...] It was undoubtedly these connections that obtained for him the post of secretary to a legation destined for the Russian and Persian courts.'[6]

The student Engelbert Kaempfer had thus become an employee of the Swedish court, a situation with which he must have been satisfied as the first step of his professional life. All the more so as his entry into the Swedish service was probably associated with the promise of a financial reward and 'the best advancement, (if he so wished) either at court or at the university of Uppsala'.[7] If that was the case, Kaempfer had adequate reasons, quite apart from his search for employment, for participating in a journey that was not without its hazards, as Olearius, for one, had shown.

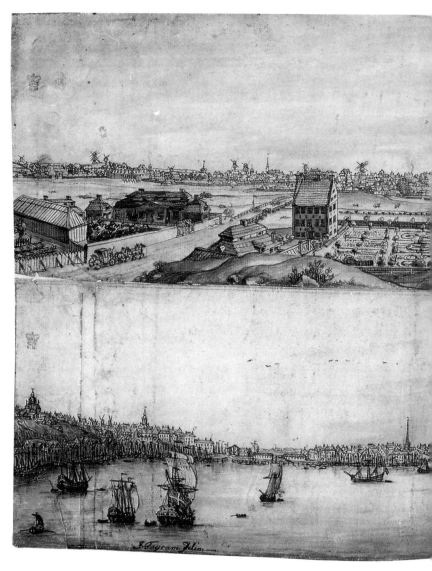

3. Views of Stockholm around 1715/25. By John Fayram.

CAROLUS XI. SUECORUM. GOTHORUM.
ET VANDALORUM. REX.

4. Charles XI, King of Sweden. He extended his hegemony around the Baltic Sea and actively promoted trade with the Orient.

Journey to Moscow

The purpose of the Swedish legation to the Persian court – like others before it – was to gain direct access to the coveted oriental raw materials, thus avoiding the added costs of the Dutch carrying trade and the long transport routes round southern Africa.[8]

As early as 1679 Charles XI had sent the envoy Ludwig Fabritius to Persia, without success.[9] With the second legation a new attempt was to be made. In addition Charles XI wished to persuade Shah Sulayman to join the European coalition against the Turks.[10] With a large retinue and bearing valuable gifts the legation set out in March 1683, again headed by the experienced Fabritius.[11]

From Stockholm it travelled to the coast, crossed over to the Åland Islands and sailed from there to Finland. In Finland it followed the direct route from Turku by way of Helsinki and Vyborg to the fort of Nyenskans (present-day St Petersburg).[12] From there it turned west towards Narva in Estonia, the last major Swedish-held town.

Beyond Narva it met with the first delay, over a matter of etiquette. On the passport the name of the Shah was entered before that of the Tsar, which led to heated arguments.[13] These were especially vexing, as the journey had to be interrupted while they were being dealt with, apart from which the stop also gave rise to additional expenses.[14]

On 8 June the legation finally crossed the Swedish-Russian border. From there it took another whole month before it was 'received' in the Moscow suburb of Sloboda, on 10 July, by a detachment of streltsy (a kind of guard regiment and police of the Tsar), or in other words escorted to its quarters: 'Now as we finally reached the suburb of Sloboda we found fifty streltsy, dressed in red and mounted, along both sides of the road. To the right in the same line stood twelve roan horses, together with a few russet ones, which were given to the equerries for the ride into the city, as well as a large white horse for the envoy, all of them with silver-mounted and gilded saddles, silken embroidered horse-cloths, bridles of silver and silk. [...] In front rode a clerk dressed in red figured taffeta, a stout individual, and the Tsar's stolnik [table companion], the lieutenant-colonel of the guard. These persons dismounted at the same time as we did and approached us, whereupon the clerk read us the Tsar's welcome address from a piece of paper. Once that was done, the colonel extended his hand to the envoy, greeted him as his appointed pristav and offered him and us the aforesaid horses. We therefore handed over the old ones for the use of our servants, who had hitherto travelled in waggons, and all mounted and rode [...] into the city.'[15]

Kaempfer's diary entries from Moscow are relatively shorter than those he wrote during the journey itself and in Persia. The outstanding event was the meeting with the two Tsars, Ivan and Peter. At the customary presentation of the credentials Kaempfer made the following observations, which show his perceptiveness and remarkable powers of description: 'Their two majesties sat not in the centre but slightly towards the right side of the hall – because of a pillar that stood in the middle – each on an episcopal throne made of silver and raised a few steps. Above each hung an icon. Over their coats they wore cloaks with figured yellow and white fields of silver, resembling chasubles; instead of sceptres they held long golden staves, curved at the top like a crozier and adorned with gems in green and other colours, as were the breast bands of the robes and the fronts of their caps. The eldest (Ivan) sat motionless with lowered eyes, largely covered by his cap, which was pulled down, while the younger, Peter, with his face raised and visible, displayed to all those standing around and in front of him his marvellous beauty through agreeable gestures and with the crimson colour of his noble line – which always flushed his cheeks when he was addressed – in such a way that, had they had before them an ordinary young girl and not an imperial personage, they would all have confessed to being infatuated.'[16]

The time in Moscow – after all, they stayed there nearly two months – was not only taken up with consultations. Kaempfer tried to see as much as possible of the life of the Russian people, though it was of course impossible for him to carry out a systematic survey in such a short time. Nevertheless, his descriptions are always lively and show how observant he was: 'on the 26th I and the interpreter were sent to Lord Golitzin, who was staying at Vorobyev Gora with their majesties the Tsars, along with other boyars and the entire court. Having taken off my overcoat, I had to sit down at table with him. The courses of food were served, starting at the top end of the table. When one had taken enough of them the boyar ordered the dish to be passed along and another to be served. As long as the boyar was eating one course, the others had to be held by the attendants until they were ordered to serve them, one after the other. The said dishes were now passed further down, until the non-equestrian nobles finished them off, standing. The food was all strongly seasoned with onions instead of garlic, the dishes were made of pewter, but the soups were served in tin-plated copper bowls. Only the boyar and his son had silver spoons, whereas we had wooden ones. During the meal beer and spirits were imbibed and afterwards mead. The first course was an uncooked sheep's head, which had been soused in vinegar, and around it were laid the last of the melons and cherries ...'[17]

He gained an insight into the exotic religious system by attending processions and services, and he described in particular detail the funeral of Hermann von Staden, the former marshal of the Holstein legation, who had settled in Moscow. He paid special attention to the burial service, as it was conducted according to the Russian Orthodox rite: 'About 12 o'clock the procession began – the priests and novices walked at the head of it, the last two each carrying a burning censer, while right at the front the coffin lid, covered with red taffeta, was carried by two men. The priests with the censers continually retraced a few steps, bowed and swung their censers towards the corpse. The latter was carried by six men who changed places with each other. As a sign of mourning they wore narrow black ribbons of taffeta like a sash over the left shoulder, hanging down on the right side. After them came the mourners in a confused mass, followed by the unmarried daughters and others on foot, both converts and other women; all the above-mentioned carried lighted candles in their hands. The corpse lay in the open coffin covered with a white taffeta cloth. In this ordered confusion the crowd went with bared heads into the church, which was indeed small but contained over eight hundred icons, of which almost half were images of Mary. Before the door to the sanctuary the corpse was set down and covered up as far as the chest, three candles being fixed at its head and three at its feet. According to the local custom, it was wrapped in a red cloth. the senior priest placed himself at the head, while at the feet a lectern was placed between the ends of the bier, on which an icon of the Annunciation was laid, turned towards the corpse. The priests distributed themselves two by two, some in lay clothing, on either side of the church in both of the large cathedrë. To the right of the door the priest laid down a large book and began to read some chapters from it, while the priests repeated their chants more than a hundred times. They also addressed the corpse by name and wished it happiness. One of those holding a censer [...] went about assiduously, alternatively fumigating the senior priest and the people. The senior priest also several times entered the sanctuary before the altar, which was a stone table with a large upright icon of Mary. When the priest who was reading from the book became tired he was relieved by another priest. When he, too, had done his duty and read aloud the chapters for which he was paid a priest brought out the certificate of testimony and indulgence, which was the size of this sheet. The senior priest read it over, to ensure that it was valid and correctly signed, then rolled it up again, as is the custom here, forced open the right hand of the corpse and placed this testimonial in it. After that the people filed in the order described above around the corpse, kissing first the aforesaid icon at its feet, then the corpse on its cold, grey mouth, before strolling in no particular order to the grave, where the corpse was entirely covered again with a silken cloth in the traditional manner, the lid was simply laid over the coffin without nails or other fastenings, and it was then lowered into the grave by two cords. Now the priest with the aforesaid icon placed himself first at the foot and then at the head of the grave and held the icon towards the corpse. The senior priest took the bowl and threw three scoops of earth on the coffin, as our people also do in Stockholm. Then the others also came up and threw three handfuls with their hands. Finally those appointed to do so covered

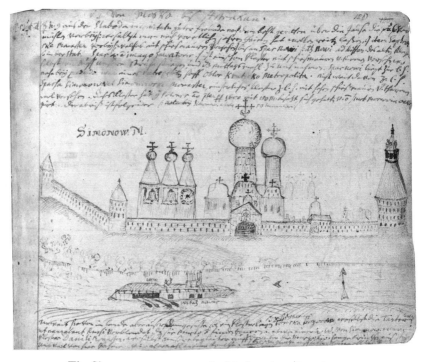

5. The Simonov monastery on the Moskva river. Drawing by Kaempfer in his Russian travel diary.

it completely. Then the crowd entered the church again, bowed before the saints and thus completed the ceremony. After that everyone either rode or otherwise accompanied the priests to the house of mourning to be further regaled.'[18]

Naturally Kaempfer did not only associate with the members of the Swedish legation but also made contact with other foreigners living in Moscow. Among the latter was the German physician in ordinary to the imperial household, Laurentius Blumentrost, the ambassadors of Denmark and the Netherlands, Horn and Baron von Keller, of whom the latter also acted on behalf of Sweden in financial matters, as well as the Germans Schertling and Engelhardt.[19] That Kaempfer also made other acquaintances beyond this circle of people is evident from the poem that he wrote about the young women of the Moscow suburb of Sloboda:

The Gourd Consumed

Ye Beauties of this town, let me explain the reason
Why on our way, forsooth, such faltering steps we take:
For to our stay with you now Heaven has set a season,
The pain of our departure the hardest heart must break!

Yet always in devotion to you we shall abide
And firmly in our minds your memory retain;
Whoso among us sets his love for you aside
He certainly will never Sloboda see again.

Well, then, you will remain here in your earthly paradise
Enjoying, as you do, a life of safety and of calm,
Your meals made all the sweeter by your merry smiling eyes,
The stars towards you wafting clouds of oriental balm.

But we to Tartars and to Persians our weary way must wend
To face the unknown dangers of the mighty Shah's domain;
Oh that our king us soon would different orders send
And bid us quickly turn our feet to Muscovy again!

Should you still think us worthy your favours to receive
Our highest wish could only be to soon return to you;
Till then in our devotion, pray, sincerely do believe –
Adieu, and trust that we remain in our affections true![20]

Although these alexandrines lack a certain polish, they do provide evidence that Kaempfer also practiced the art of occasional verse. Beyond that, however, they are a concrete example of how Kaempfer can be understood in the context of his time and his cultural environment. The title 'The Gourd Consumed',[21] which at first seems meaningless, is the key to understanding the poem: Kaempfer, who had studied not only the natural sciences but also the humanities in Danzig, Torun, Cracow and Königsberg, alluded by this title to the familiar emblem showing how love-sickness, represented by an inscription on a gourd, increases with the growth of the gourd and therefore also of the separation between the lovers. At the same time this longing is not eternal but highly mutable. Kaempfer, however, makes ironic play with the love-sickness; on the one hand he fully internalises it, while on the other hand he relativises the unconditional longing for the beauties of the Moscow suburb by the transitoriness expressed through the gourd.[22] Kaempfer does not limit himself to a straightforward account of the departure, which was indeed based on a real event, but gives it a further, ironic dimension through the symbolism and the emblematic title. His verses thus display the asso-

ciative emblematic thought patterns of educated society – and thus of
Kaempfer himself.

From Moscow to Isfahan

The normal route for travellers from Moscow to Persia took them first to
the town of Kolomna and then by boat down the Oka river to the Volga,
whose course they followed from Kazan to its estuary at Astrakhan.[23]
Even some fifty years after Olearius's journey the route had not become
any safer. Kaempfer wrote: 'Here we received further news concerning
the insecurity of our journey, as five days earlier, forty versts from here,
ten merchants were plundered, two of them shot and the rest crippled by
blows.'[24] Remarks about fight between robbers and streltsy occur repeatedly in his account. He also meticulously noted wind-strengths, the
direction of the sunrise, the distance covered and especially noteworthy
places and events. At this point, however, it should be remembered that
the surviving notes are only memoranda for the fuller treatment that
Kaempfer intended to produce after his return.[25] That explains their
laconic form and the unpolished sentences. Although a comparable
account (that of Olearius) in its published version likewise follows the
chronological order of the journey, it quite clearly reveals a subsequent
process of revision.[26]

On 1 November 1683 the Swedish legation reached Astrakhan. Here
Kaempfer made the acquaintance of a Georgian prince, who also wrote an
entry in his album.[27] As a result of this encounter it is repeatedly asserted
in the early biographies that Kaempfer had also visited Georgia; that, as
well as a conjectured journey to Egypt, is an error.[28]

From Astrakhan the party travelled on two cargo boats across the
Caspian Sea to Nisabad, where it arrived after a stormy crossing on
21 November. Due to the storm and snowfall, however, they could dis-
embark only after two days.[29] From Nisabad they travelled along the
familiar caravan road through Shemkha, Lenkoran, Astara, Resht,
Kasvin and Qum to Isfahan.[30] Kaempfer allowed himself some interesting deviations from the route. To begin with, he climbed the strangely
shaped mountain of Barmach, where the prophet Elijah is purported
to have lived. Olearius had already described the mountain but had
not ascended it.[31] Then Kaempfer made an excursion to Baku and
the naphtha wells on the Apsheron Peninsula. Not even an unpleasant
intermezzo – he and his companions were suspected in the town of being

6. A page from Kaempfer's Russian travel diary, exemplifying the condition of his manuscripts.

7. Church and gate tower in Kazan, with musical notations by Kaempfer.

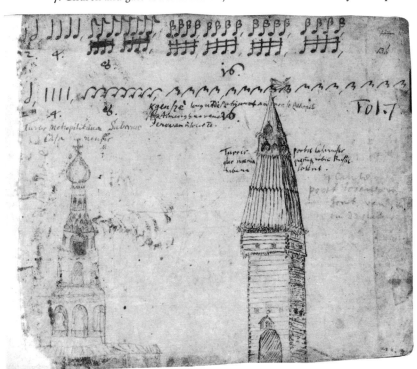

spies – deterred him from producing an accurate description and sketch of the town before he moved on. He was the first European to describe in detail the sources of the white and black naphtha (petroleum), an oil lake, a mud spring and a salt-works. He later described these phenomena at greater length than in the diaries in his *Amoenitates exoticae*.[32]

At Astara the party reached Persian territory on 3 February 1684, with the greater part of the way to the Persian capital, some 850 kilometres, still ahead of them. This distance was covered in 32 days of travelling (omitting days of rest and stops for receptions), at a rate of 23.4 kilometres a day.[33] Kaempfer broke no new ground on any of his routes in Iran, as the legation followed the main roads. The usual route passed through Resht and Kasvin and at Saveh it joined the great caravan road that ran from Erivan in a south-easterly direction towards Bandar Abbas.[34] At the time of his journey he may have been acquainted with the most significant literature on Persia, but in his diaries he exclusively and fairly frequently quotes the account of Olearius, and that in such a way as to suggest that he had brought a copy of the book with him.[35] He may already have decided by then to publish his observations in the form of a travel account and wished to compare them with those of his renowned predecessor.

The following passage illustrates how Kaempfer reacted to the new visual impressions that flooded in upon him: 'And everything one saw here [in Qum], except for the confined nature of the place, was splendid and remarkable and such as would please the eye of any curious traveller.'[36] Apart from Kaempfer's self-assessment as a 'curious' traveller, this quotation clearly reveals the open mind with which he approached the unfamiliar oriental environment. All at first appears 'remarkable' to him and serves to satisfy his curiosity. As the purpose of the travel diaries was merely to record impressions for later re-working, elaborate descriptions and characterisations will obviously not be found there.[37] On the contrary, Kaempfer jots down haphazardly everything that he comes across. We must therefore regard this recording activity, which was assisted by his gift for acute observation, as a preparation for the reworking of the material – which sadly never took place – on the lines of the *Amoenitates exoticae*.

In one respect Kaempfer may well be compared as a traveller in the last quarter of the seventeenth century with his predecessor Olearius. The description of the localities and landscapes that surround him provide hardly a clue to his own frame of mind, as they had not yet turned into a mirror for the latter, as was to become the case during the eighteenth

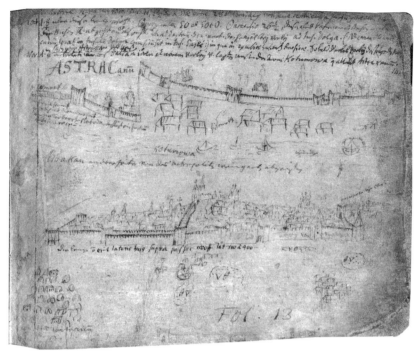

8. Sketched views of Astrakhan at the mouth of the Volga on the Caspian Sea.

9. Views of Baku and its surroundings on the Apsheron peninsula. This sheet of drawings by Kaempfer is the actual model for the engraving in the *Amoenitates exoticae*, following p.268. Kaempfer shows the different kinds of naphtha sources, the salt extracting and various noteworthy sights.

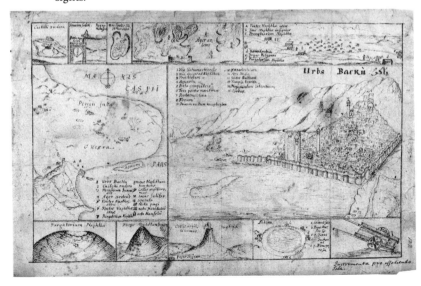

century. We read repeatedly, in topical phrases, of 'horrendous' rocks,[38] 'deserted'[39] plains and 'desolate'[40] tracts, but also of 'beautiful' fields,[41] Kaempfer as always having an eye for the agricultural. Only rarely does he provide more detailed descriptions in the diaries. Of the landscape at Lenkoran, for instance, he writes: 'The location is extremely pleasing, with the sea lying to the east, the mountains to the west, the river to the south, above the latter a fine tall forest on high, verdant ground, with oaks, walnuts, promegranates etc., all entwined with vines, and below that scattered farmhouses.'[42] He expresses himself even more emphatically about the fertile region near Rudbar: 'Everything seemed like a stage-play today. It was like being in a theatre. What more can I say? What should I admire first? Everything had already been wonderful the previous day. As soon as we rode off, or rather walked off – for the mountain paths make riding impossible – we arrived today at Rudbar over steep mountain ridges along the aforesaid river south by southwest and saw everywhere fearful gorges along whose rocky slopes houses and villages emerged in the most pleasing olive groves and gardens, in some places extending almost to the top. Here and there these evergreen olive trees alternated with orange and lemon trees and cypresses, while there were also vineyards in places. The remaining parts of the mountains, in so far as they were not craggy, were sparsely covered with green savin trees (*Juniperus sabina*). The springs of the olive-growing villages that lie along the steep mountain slopes pour their water all the way down to the river, which is everywhere very noisy and muddy.'[43]

This description, which may at first seem rather arbitrary, is rather more than that, however: it demonstrates Kaempfer's ability to vary his mode of expression (even in a rough draft) and indicates his place in the history of geographical thought. He adopts the approach, prevalent since antiquity, that regards geography as the science not primarily of nature but of humanity in its spatial relationships. Advances in instrumentation and the development of statistical and demographic studies later enabled Alexander von Humboldt to pay more attention to nature in geography than his predecessors.

Kaempfer represents an important stage in the development towards Humboldt. He loves the landscape shaped by human activity – fields, vineyards, olive groves, houses and other large buildings, all the features that we include in the concept of a 'cultural landscape'. He approaches it with sympathy and personal engagement, grasping its character rather than simply establishing quantitative facts. In his precise descriptions, along with his compass readings and fixing of geographical positions, as well as the occasional small sketches, one senses his endeavour to provide an exact record of the physical reality.[44]

In both of the passages quoted above the locality is referred to as 'pleasing' (a common baroque term for 'beautiful', 'delightful'), and in the second it actually presents itself to Kaempfer as a 'stage-play' and 'theatre'. The landscape that he favours is thus one formed by variety, a certain 'theatrical' arrangement and the predominance of a charming, fertile and subdued nature, whose terrifying aspects are relegated to the background.[45] There is no question, therefore, that Kaempfer was able to express himself in the German language. Of that he was fully capable – in the manner of an educated person of the period.

Sojourn in Isfahan. Kaempfer's parting from the Swedes

The first high point of Kaempfer's journey through Persia was the sojourn in Isfahan. After arriving there on 30 March 1684, the Swedish legation had to wait four months before being granted an audience. The reason for this was the superstitious nature of Shah Sulayman who, on the advice of the astrologers following the death of one of his concubines, refrained from appearing in public. Kaempfer therefore had time to explore the capital and its surroundings.

Nor was that all. The long wait at the political centre of the Safavid state allowed him to become acquainted with the representative aspect of the state and with part of its administration. That which was a cause of vexation to the head of delegation, Ludwig Fabritius, because of the expenses incurred, was for Kaempfer a wonderful opportunity to satisfy his passion, which was to acquire a detailed knowledge of Persian culture.

As a result, his account remains valuable even today, for thanks to his description, which was as accurate as he could make it, interesting features of the Safavid state can be comprehended through his 'outsider's view'. Although many details of its theological and political culture remained hidden from him – and the same applies equally to other travellers, both before and after him – he did grasp some of its essential social characteristics.[46]

This is how he describes the power and character of the Shah: 'The supreme head of the Iranian state is the Great King or Shah, whose office is hereditary. An idea of his exceptional position may be gained by considering two facts: the first being his vast territorial possessions, the

10. Shah Suleyman (Safi II, 1666-94). Portrait medallion in the
Amoenitates exoticae, facing p.36.

second his immense prerogatives, which exceed those of all other rulers
in Asia. Of the latter I shall merely note the most important ones. First of
all, the Great King of Iran has absolute and unlimited control over the
administration of justice. Throughout the rest of the world executive
power is circumscribed either by an acknowledged contract, i.e. by constitutional laws, or else by various informal yet insuperable limitations
and restraints. The Tsar of Russia, for example, is still restricted in the
exercise of his power by the boyars (the higher nobility), while the devout
observance of ancestral customs also restrains him from many arbitrary
acts. […] On the other hand, due to the absence of all checks, everything
is permitted to the Safavid Great King, changing the laws of the realm,
imposing new taxes, even disposing of the lives and property of every individual and his wives and children – all lies in his power, and there is no
legal protection for his subjects, high or low, against the unbridled desires
of a degenerate sovereignty.'[47]

The same applies still more to his description of the city and of the
inner palace area. Here, too, he had an advantage over other travellers in
the length of his stay in Isfahan.[48] Of the many memorable details only
three examples will be given here, namely his vivid descriptions of the
squares, the residential buildings and the gardens of Isfahan.

'The Great Square was laid out by Shah Abbas I at the same time as the

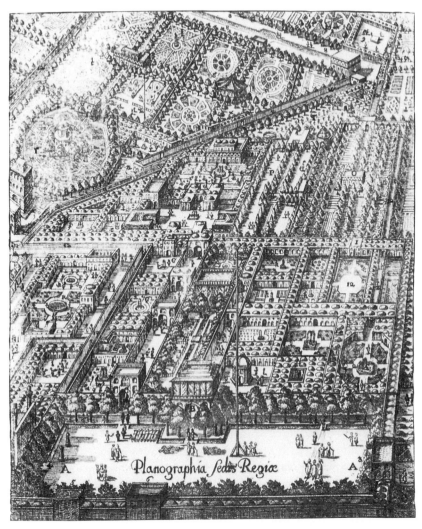

Planographia ſedis Regiæ

11. Bird's-eye view of the palace area, maidan and park in Isfahan. Kaempfer was only able to produce this painstaking depiction owing to his long sojourn in the Persian capital. Engraving in the *Amoenitates exoticae*, p.179.

adjoining royal palace and the district of Abbasabad. It far exceeds the Old Square in size and magnificence and, forming as it were a forecourt to the palace itself, I shall describe it here in more detail. The shape of the square is a rectangle of 660 paces in length (in a north-south direction) and 212 paces in width. It is surrounded by two-storeyed vaulted buildings with recesses. The upper floors are divided into small rooms that are rented out as dormitories to all sorts of foreigners as well as to prostitutes. The ground floor of this arcade serves partly as a covered walk for pedestrians but in the main to accommodate spacious bazaar stalls for shopkeepers and craftsmen, who produce and sell a variety of goods there. There is no disorder, however, but all are lodged systematically according to their professions. These neat rows of uniformly high bazaar apartments, screened by ornamental lattices, give the Shah's Square its specific attractive style. The monotony of the surrounding buildings is most pleasingly interrupted by a few prominent edifices. On the western side the royal palace of Ali Qapu serves this purpose, and not far away from there the gateway to the foyer leading to the harem. On the opposing eastern side one's eye is caught by the exceedingly elegant Mosque of Shaykh Lutf Allah, which is covered in gleaming tiles, as well as by a hall along the walls of which the curious viewer is presented with mechanical figures in warlike poses, which for a few small coins will enact vivid scenes.'[49]

'The houses of the townspeople of the Persian capital will not be described in detail. Most of them are built of air-dried mud bricks in a single storey and covered with vaults of the same material. The habitations of the poor are cramped and dark and lack an inner courtyard, while those of the affluent are grand, spacious and arranged around a square open space in the centre. The exteriors of the houses display only bare walls; all the splendour is directed inward. Particular care is devoted to the area surrounding the courtyard, which is focussed on and accentuated by a tall recess with a pointed arch, a so-called *ayvan*. The guest sits down below this *ayvan* to enjoy the view of the shimmering pond and the plants that adorn the courtyard. In the other parts of a Persian house there are windows extending to the floor; these are not filled with leaded glass, however, but with wooden lattices covered with sheets of translucent paper. The internal walls are brightly whitewashed with plaster and talc. The flat roof is adorned with carvings and blue mosaics. On the floors costly carpets are spread out, while several cushioned seats extend along the walls. Tables, footstools, benches and other such Western furniture for the chamber, kitchen and stable will be looked for in vain in a Persian house. Apart from the weaving sheds, all workshops lie open to the street, so that any passer-by can look inside them.'[50]

'In the centre of the park lies the larger of the two palaces, the Palace of Forty Columns (Chihil Sutun), which is constructed, with truly royal

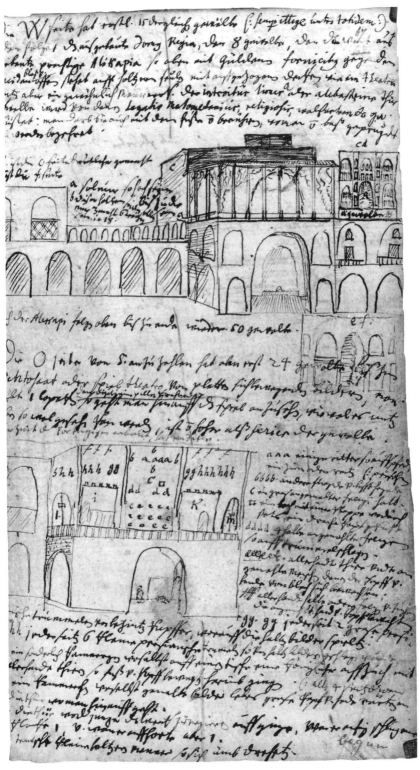

12. Isfahan – buildings along the west side of the maidan. It is clear that Kaempfer studied and recorded every single architectural detail in his sketchbook, as a basis for future publications.

splendour, partly of brick and partly of hewn stone and faces a square which is covered with polished slabs of stone and surrounded by an attractive water conduit with many gushing fountains. The palace is square in plan and provided with numerous shady rooms, arboured walks, gateways, lattices and arches, entirely in the spirit of the best Persian architecture, whose forms certainly appear strange to us. [...] The final touch is added to the splendour of the Chihil Sutun palace by a pool twenty paces wide with mirror-clear water, half of it lying behind the building and extending on either side to the end of the park. Whoever can look without pleasure at the innumerable fountains, the water fowls of variegated plumage swimming on the lake and the trees mirroring themselves in it must be as unfeeling as a log. [...] The other smaller buildings in the Park of Forty Columns, the enclosure wall, the moats or the exquisite gardens I shall refrain from describing more closely.'[51]

It should be apparent how precisely Kaempfer wishes to transmit what he has seen to the European reader and the extent to which he attempts to find appropriate ways of describing the characteristic features of Persian town planning and daily life, without immediately lapsing into judging them by European standards yet also without wishing to deny the exotic aspects of Persian culture.

The same could also be said of his illustrations. Due to his skills as a draughtsman, they create not an oriental fantasy world but a realistic image of the conditions of that period.[52] At the same time one should not overlook the fact that Kaempfer only became increasingly accomplished as a draughtsman during the course of his journeys. In the drawings from Russia, and partly even in those from Persia, there is still an awkwardness typical of the amateur. In Kaempfer's sketch of the maidan, for instance, one can clearly see the various elements of the gateway despite the fact that it was obviously drawn very rapidly. In the overall design of the square the perspective and proportions are not entirely consistent with each other. This becomes problematic in its transposition by the engraver Donop. He faithfully reproduces everything that the author has outlined for him but falls into the same error of perspective with regard to the gateway. Worst of all, the threshold with the protuberance that must not be touched becomes a small ornamental pyramid in the engraving! On the other hand, the human activity in the square, with which Kaempfer was entirely unconcerned in his drawing, represents a veritable 'operatic Orient' in the engraving, with all the elements of the East as imagined by Europeans. A crowd of Persians stand around in the classic pose with the

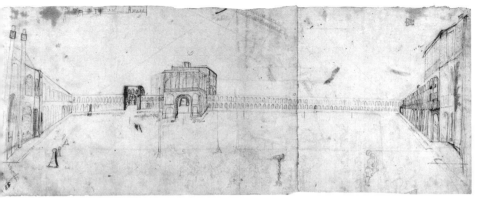

13. Isfahan – the maidan, partial view of the west side. This large sheet shows an initial attempt by Kaempfer to show the great square in perspective. Compare this with the plate in the *Amoenitates exoticae*, following p. 170.

14. 'The Great Messczit', the great mosque of Isfahan (in the *Amoenitates* Kaempfer writes 'Mesdsjed') situated at the southern end of the maidan.

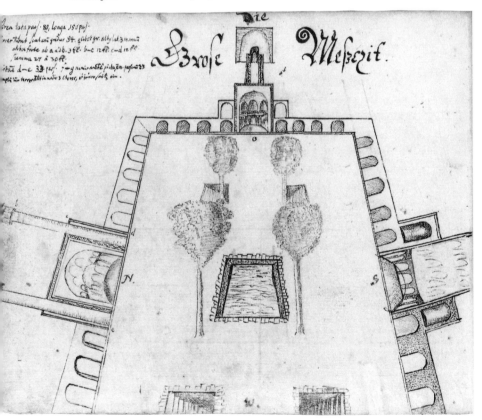

weight on one leg – familiar from European portraits of rulers – while some promenade formally up and down; all are identically depicted in turbans and cloaks, merchants and opium smokers being posed with equal elegance. And looming above the whole scene are the victor's garland, the eagle's wings and baroque 'glory haze' of the Shah. Genuine Persian elements are here inextricably mingled with European notions to produce a concept of life in the capital of the Persian realm that can scarcely correspond to what Kaempfer actually saw.

Fortunately Kaempfer became acquainted, in the person of Fr Raphael du Mans, with a distinguished expert on Persian affairs who represented the interests of the King of France in Isfahan as head of the Capuchin monastery there.[53] Having resided in Persia for decades and occasionally acted as an interpreter at the court of Shah Abbas II, he had an intimate acquaintance with the language and customs of the country.[54] Kaempfer received from him not only linguistic tuition, as shown by some notes on Turkish grammar preserved among his papers[55] but also an introduction to Persian history.[56] It was with reluctance that Kaempfer parted from him, and their correspondence, though it did not continue for very long, proves that there was a friendly disposition and intellectual harmony between them.

The outcome of the Swedish mission is well known. It did not achieve its aim of a coalition between Sweden and the Persian state against the Turks, but it marked the beginning of a commercial relationship between Sweden and Persia that flourished until 1700, in spite of the fact that it could be conducted only by Persian and Armenian and not by Swedish merchants.[57] Among the competitors of the Swedes was the Dutch East India Company, which controlled a not inconsiderable part of the trade with Persia and naturally defended this strongly against its rivals.

5. *Kaempfer's enlistment in the Dutch East India Company*

Journey to the Persian Gulf

Why did Kaempfer decide not to return home with the Swedes? At this point we must again address the question that arose at the very beginning of his career. It became clear that his plans for his life and profession cannot be defined by the notion of 'becoming an explorer'.[1] What then were the reasons that led such a rationally functioning man, who can hardly be described as an adventurer, to commit himself to the uncertainty of further travels, at the end of which he had no guarantee of permanent employment? One can assume that, during his stay in Isfahan, Kaempfer had become aware of the general conditions of travelling and living in contemporary Persia and Asia and had no illusions about comfort and the chances of survival. Information provided by the well-informed Fr Raphael is also likely to have contributed to his decision.[2]

Although his letters of application to influential members of the Dutch East India Company cannot be taken literally in every particular, as he of course argued his case in such a way as to win their support, there are two passages in his writings where reasons are stated which quite closely reflect his real considerations.

One of them is the passage in the introduction to his work on Japan where he writes: 'Germany was still being troubled simultaneously by the most Christian and the least Christian foe when the Swedish legation, in whose service I was employed, was discharged from the Persian court. I therefore found it more advisable to undertake a further journey and rather expose myself to voluntary discomfort than to return to my fatherland and submit myself to its general misfortune and the conditions of war forced upon it by its enemies.'[3]

Kaempfer makes no reference to the offer from the Swedish court (see above, p. 15) either here or elsewhere. Should one conclude from this that it was perhaps not as firm as it may at first have appeared? Kaempfer's return to Sweden would not in any way have confronted him with the distressing economic and political conditions in his homeland, where on the

37

15. View of Isfahan. Engraving in the *Amoenitates exoticae*, following p. 162. In the style of the period the view is somewhat idealised but clearly shows the location of Isfahan on the high plateau below a mountain range.

16. The bridges of Isfahan. Engraving in the *Amoenitates exoticae*, following p. 166. Kaempfer describes the bridges because of their age and their remarkable and in parts even magnificent architecture.

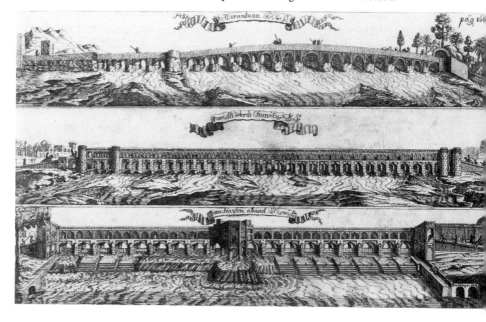

one hand fear of the Turks was increasing (it was only finally banished by the peace of Karlowitz in 1699) and on the other hand Louis XIV was intervening on a massive scale, i.e. militarily, in the European power struggle. Moreover, not having completed his studies, he could hardly have expected any position of real importance in Lemgo, whatever the relationship was between his father and the town council.[4]

It is tempting to conclude, therefore, that in Kaempfer's view the journey with the legation – which had offered him his first employment as well as an opportunity for interesting travel – had become a blind alley. In Isfahan itself the possibilities for a foreigner to support himself for any length of time were limited. 'Flight ahead' was therefore almost unavoidable for Kaempfer. But what options did he have? The answer is given by the following passage in his writings:

'However, I was persuaded, on the advice of the venerable Capuchin Father du Mans, to accept the invitation from the Dutch admiral, who was blockading the bay of Hormuz with his fleet.'[5] Kaempfer had already made the acquaintance of Dutch East India Company officials in Isfahan – including Herbert de Jager – who had clearly passed on his application to a higher authority. Admiral Casembrood, to whom he refers, had brought a small fleet to anchor before Bandar Abbas on 3 June 1684. The purpose of this action was to exert pressure on Shah Sulayman to change the terms of trade in favour of the Dutch and the Company.[6] The latter presented itself as a great commercial power, strong enough not only to present demands but also to enforce them.

Shortly afterwards, however, Casembrood died and Kaempfer therewith lost a patron. This was a misfortune that may have affected his career to a not inconsiderable degree. In that situation Fabritius used his influence on behalf of his secretary. Kaempfer finally succeeded in December 1684 in obtaining from the Director Justus van Heuvel an appointment as a senior surgeon in the service of the Company. Nevertheless, he had to remain in Isfahan for almost another year without pay before he was able to travel with a caravan to Bandar Abbas.[7]

The Dutch East India Company was known as an employer that sought and recruited its employees all over Europe, from rank and file soldiers to scholars and administrators. Kaempfer therefore looked for the best opportunity available to him in his situation. That was the Company, which could take him if not to Europe then to the legendary India. Just as little as Kaempfer was prepared for the art treasures and natural wealth of Persia did he have any thoughts, while he was in Sweden, of visiting

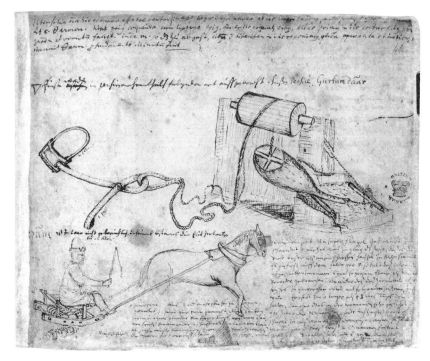

17. Equipment for drawing water, seen by Kaempfer in Persia.

India or far less Japan. That his voyage would finally take him by way of Batavia to Japan he could surely neither have known nor even guessed at this point in time. Thus each phase of his travels arose out of the preceding one and was in no way planned. It is therefore all the more remarkable – and that is Kaempfer's real achievement – to what good account he managed to turn each new situation.

The journey of approximately one thousand kilometres to Bandar Abbas in December 1685 was interrupted by two particular high points: the inspection of the fabled ruins of Persepolis and the visit to Shiraz, the city of the poets Hafiz and Sa'di. He examined both places thoroughly, though he was allowed only a short time to describe and draw Persepolis and Naqsh-i Rustam. (He abandoned the idea of visiting the more distant tomb of Cyrus, the founder of the Persian empire, at Pasargadae 'due to the uncertainty', presumably about the way there.[8]) During three days of sustained activity of drawing and description he attempted to master the complex structures and their strange and fascinating sculptural ornamentation. He thus writes, among other things, of Persepolis: 'The entrance is at the front, near its western end, with a double staircase converging on a forecourt. On one side 55 steps lead up on the right to a landing and from there 58 steps in the opposite direction, leftward, to the forecourt, which is 24 paces long and eight paces wide. On the other side the staircase leads first to the left, then to the right up on to the platform. From the latter one proceeds by two steps up on to the base level of the entire complex. The steps are made of marble of the same colour as the walls and in most cases twelve have been carved from a single block. The length of each step is eight paces, the width a foot and a half and the height scarcely more than a hand. This design was chosen so that one could comfortably reach the terrace even on horseback. [...] On the terrace are several very splendid edifices, though they are now so ruined and lie in such confusion that one can barely make out the identity, the ground plan or even the number of the buildings. The splendid effect is produced mainly by the mass of enormous columns that appear to have supported the roof, as well as the ornamental doorways that surround the buildings. Of these, some are made of white and others of dark red marble, both of the hardest and most glossy kind, and of such huge, specially selected blocks that, however large the columns or doorways were, at most three or four and seldom more were used in their construction. Added to this everywhere is the fine quality of the various sculptured emblems and images, both sacred and profane.'[9]

Of the reception hall of Xerxes he writes, among other things: 'This is the prime and most important building of the entire complex, with a splendid group of columns, generally referred to by the Persians as Chihil Minar (Forty Columns). For ease of reference we shall call the edifice the central hall. It is raised above the general level of the terrace by dark walls, a foot and a half in height, so that it presents the appearance of yet another, higher platform. It is square in plan, extending about 140 paces from east to west, i.e. to the end of the palace terrace, and further from north to south. At the front, which lies on the northern side, it has four ascents or staircases. The first two are placed opposite each other at the centre of the front side, so that one staircase rises from west to east and the other from east to west. If one steps back 40 paces on either side of these, one discovers two other recessed staircases arranged in the same way [...]. The sculptures are arranged in two tiers separated by an intervening strip of wall, from west to east. Both tiers show a solemn religious or triumphal procession that extends from the staircase by the plain across to the one

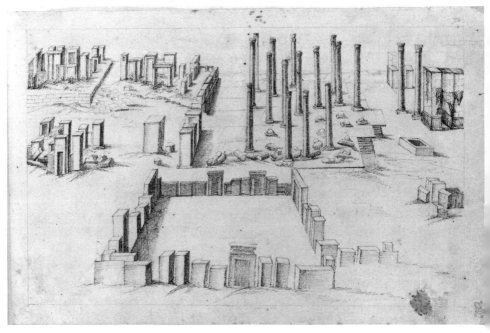

18. View of Persepolis from the east; in this sketch Kaempfer has not yet quite succeeded in depicting its true dimensions.

19. Various sketches made at Persepolis. It is obvious with what care Kaempfer records every measurement to enable him to represent the proportions when reworking the material for publication.

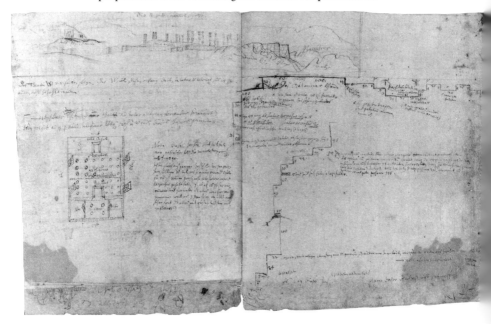

facing the mountain, in other words from west to east. The upper tier is
headed by a nobleman, borne in a two-wheeled chariot drawn by two men
as if by draught animals. In the lower tier a winged lion fights with a
single-horned bull. Close by a slab has been attached with 24 lines of text
in the wedge-shaped script peculiar to this palace. From the terrace to the
eastern staircase the frieze along the base displays nothing but archers,
holding a spear in their right hand and carrying a quiver over their
shoulder, dressed in loose robes, some with a head-dress resembling a
crown. Such a line of archers decorates the walls of all the staircases.'[10]

This is not the place to deal with the inaccuracies and errors of
Kaempfer, caused by his surveying these ruins without preparation.
More important is the nature of the account. Kaempfer hardly ever in-
dulges in dubious speculations but essentially records what is actually
there. Only on the basis of his illustrations did an image of this historic
site emerge that would make further investigations possible. His edited
description in the *Amoenitates exoticae* makes it quite clear that he criticised authors, with justification, only if they gave accounts that contra-
dicted his own experience.[11] His role may therefore well be described as
that of a field researcher who, as a first step, attempts to record the facts.

His illustrations in the *Amoenitates exoticae* were sharply criticised by
Cornelis de Bruijn in his *Reizen over Moskovie*. The most controversial
point that De Bruijn dealt with in this work was the question of the
accurate representation of the localities.[12]

Kaempfer's main achievement, compared to his predecessors della
Valle, Thévenot and Chardin, was that in such a short time he produced
drawings of Persepolis that added a number of new details to the previously known representations.[13] Even if he erred in regard to the proportions of the palaces, his drawings never generalise but are, on the
contrary, rich in details and figures and surpass those of previous visitors.[14] It is not surprising that he was partly mistaken in his interpretation
of the figures portrayed in the reliefs, as knowledge of the ancient Iranian
culture was very limited in Europe. That would change only during the
late eighteenth and nineteenth centuries with Niebuhr, Crawfurd, Fin-
layson, Porter and Morier. Ritter's *Erdkunde* is also a significant milestone
in the advance of knowledge about ancient Iran.[15] In assessing Kaempfer's
achievement it is, of course, vitally important to know his drawings and
not merely the engravings and woodcuts in the *Amoenitates exoticae*, an
option that was not available to his contemporaries. Only a comparison
of the drawings made directly on the spot with the copies judged to be

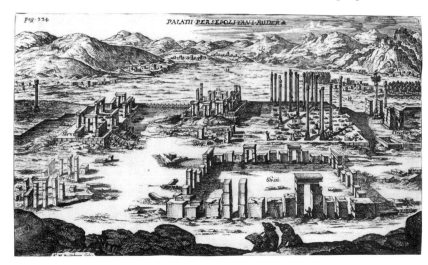

20. View of Persepolis in the *Amoenitates exoticae*, following p.334. By the figure in the foreground Kaempfer indicates himself, though without any attempt at portraiture, as the artist – a common motif in the seventeenth century.

21. Sketch of a relief at Naqsh-i Rustam. It shows king Ardashir receiving the ring of lordship from the god Ormazd. Kaempfer interprets this as the mythical hero Rustam with other persons.

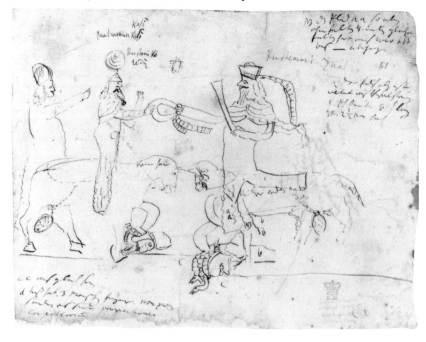

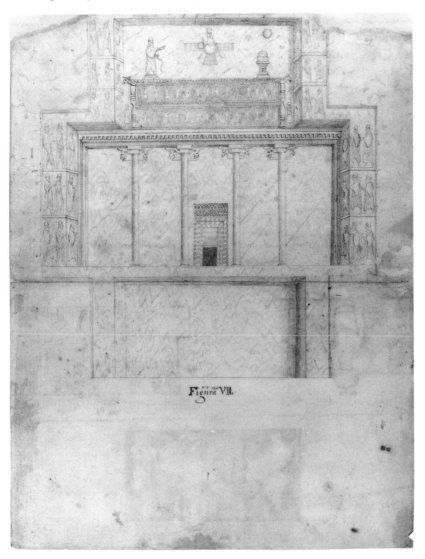

22. Large-scale view of the entrance to the supposed grave of king Xerxes. Preliminary drawing for the engraving in the *Amoenitates exoticae*, p.313. Kaempfer praises its magnificence and fineness of execution.

acceptable by the engraver Brandshagen will reveal how close Kaempfer got to the actual reality, though of course even his perception could not be 'objective'.[16]

Correctly assessing the difficulty of depicting the huge complex of ruins, Kaempfer commented: 'Should anyone wish to produce an exact representation of the sculptures, inscriptions, dimensions, ornaments and everything else worthy of note, he would scarcely find sufficient time if he stayed two months on the spot. I shall conscientiously convey as much as I could record of these things in the space of three consecutive days, during which I allowed myself no time to eat.'[17]

Despite these problems, his chapter on Persepolis is regarded as a notable advance in the exploration of this historic site, and even Niebuhr accords Kaempfer a place of honour: 'I cannot, however, approve of the severity with which de Bruyn criticises Chardin's drawings. In my judgement, he himself made many sketches on the spot with a pencil and only drew them later in ink, whereby much became unrecognisable. It would therefore have been better had he not published his remarks about Chardin and Kaempfer; for in these he often accuses those travellers of errors in order to defend his own faulty drawings.'[18]

Apart from the representations of the places themselves, Kaempfer's drawing of the curious written characters that he found there is important for the whole future debate on the cuneiform script. He was the first after della Valle and Chardin to copy a whole inscribed slab – in the brief time available to him it was not possible for him to do more: 'In reality the copying of a single inscription was such an incredibly wearisome labour, especially as the slabs are fixed so high up that one could not escape the sun. I was finally forced to abandon the idea of copying the other slabs.'[19] It was he, moreover, who was the first to coin the striking and appropriate designation 'wedge shaped'[20] for these characters, whereas they had previously been referred to as 'nail writing'.[21] As early as 1704 De Bruijn did indeed copy six inscribed slabs, but he did not contribute decisively to the deciphering of the script. It was thus only in 1765 that Niebuhr finally succeeded, with his unsurpassed drawings of the inscriptions, in making a lasting contribution to their decipherment. However, travellers like Kaempfer, Chardin and De Bruijn laid the foundations on which later scholars could build.[22]

Before reaching Bandar Abbas one still had to pass through Shiraz, where Sa'di and Hafiz had lived and worked. In describing their poetry Kaempfer must have benefitted from the tuition in Persian that he had

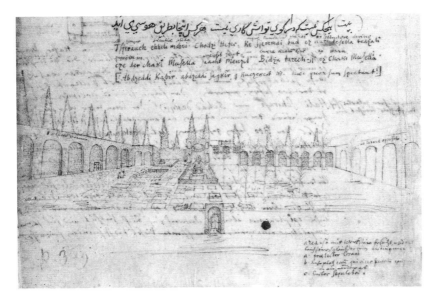

23. The tomb of the poet Hafiz. Preliminary drawing for the engraving in the *Amoenitates exoticae*, p.369. This also demonstrates how much more accurate Kaempfer's drawing was than the engraving.

24. Sketch of Bugun (Beyan) in the mountains north of Bandar Abbas, where Kaempfer convalesced.

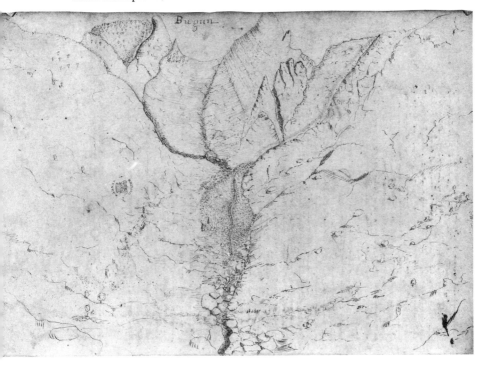

received from Fr Raphael.[23] But if Kaempfer had thought that he would soon be able to embark at Bandar Abbas and see the fabled India he had deceived himself. He was also aware that, owing to the unhealthy climate, a sojourn on the coast of the Persian Gulf would be an ordeal, if nothing worse. He writes in his diary: '28 Dec. [1685] to Gombrun or, as the Persians call it, Bandar Abbas [...] through marshy and stony hill country, surrounded by mountains [...]. [...] From the Band-Ali caravanserai e[astwards] 3 farsangs [a Persian measure of distance] through withered palm gardens and sparse shrubs to the town of Gombrun, the port of Hormuz, which is world-famous and praised as blessed throughout Persia but is in reality the most barren, driest, hottest, most poisonous, unhealthiest, most cursed place in the world and nearest to Hell [...]. Here, on first entering our residence, we found the black corpse of an old servant in the doorway: a lamentable result of this hellish atmosphere; whom, after greeting our fellow-lodgers, we helped to bury and began our business among the dead.'[24]

Kaempfer's pessimism proved well founded in every respect. And yet he would be forced to endure here until 1688. Like his colleagues in the Dutch trade mission, he fell ill. After a short period of leave, notwithstanding, he had to resume work immediately. Despite a letter in which Kaempfer gave a detailed account of his desperate state of health, his superior van Heuvel granted him no further leave.[25]

He was finally rescued from this apparently hopeless situation by the intervention of the Dutch East India Company's special commissioner for India, Wibrand Lycochthon. Thanks to the latter's influence a substitute was found for Kaempfer and he was able to travel to the health resort of Bugun, situated some hundred kilometres north of Bandar Abbas. This saved Kaempfer's life and he was restored to his former vigour. As a convalescent in a salubrious atmosphere he also became capable again of active observation and work.

In these surroundings Kaempfer wrote a piece that he later included in the *Amoenitates exoticae* but which can also be regarded as an independent work and is of great value for the cultural history of southern Persia. It is his treatise on the date palm, 'Palma arbor'.[26] In the *Amoenitates* he called it 'Phoenix persicus', with reference to its classical metaphorical sense: 'It is surely from the *Phoinix*, or *Palma dactylifera*, the noblest of all trees, sacred to Phoebus, most graceful, auspicious and long-lived, that the feathered Phoenix derives its origin and its name.'[27] His description of the plant is indeed unproductive in as much as he, too, was unable to settle

25. Some scenes of date harvesting and Persian farming. Kaempfer has depicted every stage of the date harvest in a similar engraving in the *Amoenitates exoticae*, following p.710, and of agriculture in the same work, p.680.

26. Drawings of details of the date palm and its fruits. Compare these with the engravings in the *Amoenitates exoticae*, following pp.672 and 696.

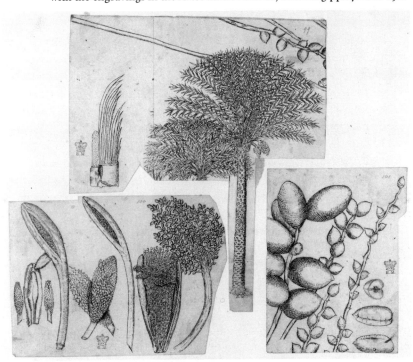

the question of its sexuality.[28] Nevertheless his precise botanical description made this text a standard work that remained unsurpassed until the publication of *Phoenix dactylifera* by Carl Friedrich von Martius in 1850.[29]

Kaempfer did not, however, restrict himself to merely listing the botanical properties of the plant but went beyond that to deal exhaustively with its origin and the explanation of its name. He describes the conditions required for its growth and harvesting, etc. At this point his account changes into a treatise on cultural or economic geography. Here he spreads his net widely, enquiring into every activity associated with the cultivation of the date palm: no significant aspect escapes Kaempfer's attention, from the artificial fertilisation of the female trees, the harvesting of the dates and their processing, through the details of the journey to the date gardens of those with no groves of their own, to the tenancy agreements and the celebrations held after work or at harvest festivals. In addition, he benefits here from his wide-ranging interests as a student; thanks to his musical pursuits he is also able at this juncture to cover an aspect that is important in the East, namely the background music on festive occasions. He thus describes exactly what music was played, which instruments were used and which dances were performed, and he rounds his account off graphically with an illustration of the instruments.

The following short extracts from the account, which is so rich in content and detail, can provide only a slight impression of his narrative skill. Of the festivals and ceremonies, for example, he writes: 'The contracts having been concluded with a religious blessing, and with all cares thus banished from the world – to what should the relieved guests now aspire, what else could they desire with their newly earned wealth but cheerful entertainments, jovial company and a festive meal? Should you feel inclined to participate in these, dear reader, I shall invite you to the table, decked by Ceres herself, and present to you all the pleasures in which the happy inhabitants of this land and their guests indulge themselves for four or five months on end with the greatest delight. [...] The food is as simple as the drink [water]: it consists of dates served not in accordance with the more ostentatious Persian customs, in bowls made of gold, brass or stone, but laid on wooden platters called *tabaq*, which suffice for the needs of those present. O pure, wholesome food, without spices or superfluous display! O happy, unassuming guests! Yet in order that these rustic festivities should not lack the signs of outward merriment there are also present actors, poets, dancers, musicians, and whatever else the heart desires. Now a *sa'ir* or singer presents the amorous joys and pain of the

27. Sketches of Persian musical instruments. In the chapter 'Lusus et recreationes' of the *Amoenitates exoticae* Kaempfer also describes the entertainments after the date harvest, which included musical performances; compare these with the engraving on p.741.

heroine Layla and her beloved Majnun in ingenious rhymes; now a *qissah khvan* or story-teller describes the strength, the deeds and battles of the Persian Hercules, Rustam son of Sal, or the mastery in javelin-throwing and other accomplishments of Bahram son of Yazdagird. [...] When the sun sets and the relaxed limbs begin to feel chilly dances are sometimes also performed. [...] But the music to which the dancers move their feet – how strange it sounds! How enjoyable are the dissonances and the diversity of instruments! First I would mention the oboes, *sarna'i*, whose grunting tones penetrate the ear before all others. These are accompanied by single-toned small bells similar to ours or by large cymbals called *sinj*, which are shaped like dinner-plates but with a smaller base and wider rim; they have handles on their convex side with which to hold and strike them together. Time is kept with tambourines, either the oblong barrel-shaped *danbal*, borrowed from India, or the *duhul*, introduced from Europe, to whose beat our soldiers march. There are also drums so large that they cannot be carried around.'[30]

Having described the multiplicity of instruments, Kaempfer turns his attention to the activities during the date harvest: 'No one should think, however, that these rustic people are only busy amusing themselves in the palm groves and maintain a kind of carefree frogs' concert throughout the summer. They actually devote a couple of hours each day to the dates, the owners to those on their own trees, the strangers to those on the rented ones. At daybreak they collect the fallen dates, then pick the ripe ones from the trees or shake them off and dry them, compress them and diligently carry out all the other work that has to be done, as I have described above. During the intervening breaks, however, and after the ending of the day's work they relax with dancing and music. Nor do the poorer ones, who are excluded from the date harvest, go idle; they likewise labour for their livelihood. In the morning they busy themselves "gleaning" dates [gathering fallen ones] – if I may call it that – and at dusk they catch locusts, which fly about in large numbers at that time. They either capture them with nets or singe them on the trees. They place the fresh catch in clay pots and roast it with some salt over a fire, stirring it with a ladle. Others prefer to boil them in water in order to remove their pungent smell. After removing their wings and legs they still their hunger – in my opinion a disgusting, loathsome diet. One can only assume that John the Baptist's emaciation was due to this vile lenten fare, on which he sustained himself in the desert. Although one might substitute these insects (of which there are multitudes in the desert) for the quails with which the Israelites are supposed to have been fed from heaven in the desert, one should be careful not to do any violence to the Hebrew text of Holy Scripture.'[31]

Lastly, in a concluding chapter he summarises the usefulness of the date palm in respect of its personal, medicinal and magico-mystical applications. In this way a microcosm of an economic region in the Middle East emerges for the reader within the space of a few pages. In achieving this, Kaempfer's account is never dry and didactic; on the contrary, he endeavours to combine the multiplicity of facts into a clear and vivid representation of the culture. The structure of the text shows how closely linked, in his view, are the natural factors and human activities, and how he already devotes somewhat more space to physical nature alongside the traditionally extensive human element.[32] Without unduly stressing the inherent tendency in the treatise, it may be regarded as one of the earliest steps in the direction of Alexander von Humboldt, whose researches more than a century later were explicitly based on precisely that general approach.[33] In southern Persia, apart from the *Palma arbor*, Kaemper wrote shorter treatises on the harvesting of asafoetida and the 'true mummy', two medicinal drugs[34] widely used in the East, as well as on the St John's Christians [Mandaeans],[35] on electric rays[36] and on the Medina worm.[37]

In attempting an overall assessment of Kaempfer's Persian notes, one has to remember that he did not complete everything he planned. However, the finished parts of the *Amoenitates exoticae* provide a fair idea of how he might have worked up the rest of his material. In writing his own account he paid careful regard to the existing literature on the subject, meaning above all the travel narratives of della Valle, Tavernier, Olearius, Thévenot and Chardin, from whose texts he extracted the best information available on Persia at that time.[38] Apart from the printed sources, he later had access to the description of Persia written by Raphael du Mans as well as other excerpts.[39] In addition, after his return to Westphalia he obtained literature through his friend Daniel Parvé which he would not have been able to acquire at all in Lieme and perhaps only with great difficulty within Westphalia.[40] He thus wrote off, among other things, for the works of Thévenot, Foris, Alpinus and Hyde.[41]

Apart from that, the following statement in the preface to the *Amoenitates exoticae* provides a clue to his working method: 'I have introduced nothing drawn from my own imagination, nothing with the imprint of the study, or the reek of lamp oil. Nor have I re-heated cabbage boiled by others, unless the context requires it, but restrict myself to describing that which is either new or has not been thoroughly and fully recorded by others.'[42] His aim thus seems to be not the encyclopaedic accumulation of data but primarily the presentation of such facts and events as had not yet been described at the time of his journey. Although he claims, entirely in accordance with conventional modesty, that his 'little work' is merely a foretaste of what is to follow,[43] his pride in his achievement is palpable in the sentences quoted above. At the same time, however, these sentences cannot disguise the fact that in the *Amoenitates exoticae* he cites and makes use of altogether more than 150 works on his subject by other scholars. Even if he intended to write other books, at least this first one was to display his erudition and gain for him a commensurate status. A passage in a letter from Herbert de Jager to Kaempfer makes the expectations of the period very clear: 'I can therefore but foresee, dear Sir, that You will return with a rich harvest, that will most gloriously immortalise Your name throughout Europe.'[44] In that context it is entirely understandable that he was angry about the inferior engravings of Brandshagen, as they might have advertised his achievement more emphatically than anything else.[45]

If one reads the Persian sections of the *Amoenitates* with this in mind, the structure of his work becomes clear. His prolonged stay in Isfahan enables him to provide a detailed account of the administration, of the life at court and of the capital itself (part one). In the second part he lists particular sights: a tower of hunting spoils in Isfahan, the ancient sites of Persepolis and Naqsh-i Rustam, the graves of the poets Hafiz and Sa'di at Shiraz. The fourth part is entirely devoted to his account of the date palm and its cultivation. The disjointedness of the work is only apparent; its connecting element is in fact novelty.

It is obvious even from Kaempfer's sketches that his aim is to provide a faithful record of the natural features of Persia as well as of its cultural phenomena: 'If he was to turn his Persian experiences into a book he could distinguish himself from his predecessors only by a scientific mode of enquiry.'[46] Hüls is thus correct in emphasising the value of the drawings made on the spot, which underline the vividness of Kaempfer's descriptions.[47]

It must have been with relief and thankfulness that Kaempfer received news in the spring of 1688 of the arrival of the Dutch ship that brought his patron Lycochthon and Director Verdunck to inspect the trading post and at the same time to bring Director van Heuvel to account 'for his brutality and insolent conduct'.[48] From them Kaempfer obtained the

28. Sketch of Hormuz (Bandar Abbas) on the Persian Gulf, where Kaempfer worked between 1685 and 1688 as a physician at the Dutch factory. Compare this with the splendid view in the *Amoenitates exoticae*, p.759.

longed-for permission to embark for India. There were apparently problems even with that, however, for Kaempfer wrote somewhat tortuously that only 'after much solicitation and effort had it seemed not impossible' that he would be allowed to travel on the ship.[49]

India

After taking on a cargo of Persian merchandise the *Coppelle* of Rotterdam set course on 30 June 1688 for Muscat in the Horn of Arabia and then put out to sea for Southern India.[50] On 9 August she reached Tuticorin on the Malabar Coast of India, where three weeks were spent discharging her cargo.[51] On 1 September the voyage continued to Point de Galle in Ceylon. From there the ship sailed to the Coromandel Coast in India, rounded Ceylon once again and returned to the Malabar Coast.

Kaempfer naturally did not have as much time during the voyage round India and Ceylon as he had had in Persia. Yet even here he made a number of interesting observations which were later incorporated into the *Amoenitates*. These included observations on the judicial ordeal on the Malabar Coast[52] and on various endemic diseases such as hydrocele and elephantiasis.[53] His attention was not drawn only to the local culture, however. He also observed the Europeans, whether they were employees of the Company or Portuguese Jesuits, among some of whom he noted an ignorance that astonished him.[54] All in all, however, he was probably disappointed, as Meier-Lemgo correctly suggests, that the 'fabled India' remained closed to him. He had, after all, written proudly to a student friend before he left Persia: 'I shall now travel from here by way of the noblest courts in India to China and trust to the fortune with which heaven has blessed my art, which is highly esteemed at all Asian courts.'[55] In that situation, where his wealth of experience brought him offers to stay in India, he was close to homesickness. But 'the latest news about the conditions at home [caused] me to hesitate again'.[56] Before his final departure for south-east Asia he thus again reflected on his professional and social prospects in Westphalia, which must have seemed to him rather limited as a medical student who had not (as yet) graduated.

Java

In the autumn of 1689 the ship sailed away from the Indian subcontinent and, after crossing the Bay of Bengal, passed Sumatra and reached Batavia in Java.[57]

Here a botanical paradise awaited him, though he was not the first to collect unknown plants there and describe and catalogue them. By the seventeenth century not only Java but the whole of south-east Asia was already the goal of everyone who was interested in botany. As early as 1678 Adriaan van Rheede tot Drakensteen had published the two-volume work *Hortus Malabaricus* on the flora of south-east Asia, while Georg Eberhard Rumpf of Hanau (whose name was latinised as Rumphius) had succeeded, after years of labour, in compiling the *Herbarium Amboinense*, on the flora of the Moluccas,[58] which even during his lifetime gained for him the title of a 'Plinius Indicae'. Kaempfer also shared his botanical interests with Herbert de Jager[59] and Andreas Cleyer.[60]

Batavia (present-day Jakarta) was the administrative centre of the Dutch East India Company in Asia. Information flowed together here from all over the vast Asian region, it was here that decisions were taken about trade and personnel and from here that the ships left regularly for Europe, India and the Far East. Although Kaempfer's botanical studies were productive, his professional situation became disagreeable again. He apparently became involved in an intrigue and was marginalised by his superior, the surgeon general in Batavia: 'he ordered matters in such a way that I obtained neither of the two vacant posts at the hospital, those of chief surgeon and apothecary; in the absence of an advocate to speak for me, a defenceless stranger, [...] I had to learn the truth that much depends

29. Hendrik Adriaan van Rheede tot Drakensteen. Engraving, about 1684, attributed to Pieter Stevenz. van Gunst. Kaempfer sent him his dissertation on the date palm. From: Johannes Heniger, *Hendrik Adriaan van Reede tot Drakenstein (1636-1691) and Hortus Malabaricus, a contribution to the history of Dutch colonial botany*. Rotterdam, Boston, 1986.

on the time in which and the people among whom an able man finds him-self.'[61] That Kaempfer was right has been shown by Eva Kraft's study of the sources: during 15 years Strijckersbergh promoted only three sur-geons to chief surgeon, and he was clearly also a difficult man to deal with.[62]

Apart from arousing one's natural sympathy for the diligent Kaempfer in his adversity, two things emerge from the above perhaps somewhat undiplomatic letter to the burgomaster of Amsterdam, the renowned Nicolaas Witsen. First, as an employee of the Company, Kaempfer appears to have had 'false' friends, above all of the kind who took an interest in scientific matters but who were unable or unwilling to do any-thing for the German physician. And second, he seems to have intended, as he writes in the same letter, to remain in Batavia and later return to Europe ('if a suitable position should become available to me there').[63]

6.   *The voyage to Siam and Japan*

Visit to Ayutthaya

It then so happened that the position of physician at Deshima, the Dutch East India Company's establishment in Japan, became vacant. Kaempfer seized the opportunity. The chance of a visit to the almost provocatively isolated Japan was no doubt preferable to his life in Batavia, which may not have been strenuous but was professionally unattractive. Yet his motive was by no means 'to conquer an entirely new field for science in Japan'.[1] It was primarily a matter of securing his material existence. He was also, however, regarded as qualified to collect plants in Japan – though the importance of this task can only be understood if one thinks of Rumpf, who spent his whole life collecting plants on Amboina for the Company. Only information on the natural conditions of each region provided the power to control future areas of exploitation and markets.

Since it was first discovered Japan had been the object of the most varied endeavours and desires. Beginning with Marco Polo, who had already called attention to the immense supplies of gold in the country, interest later became focussed on spreading Christianity there and sub-sequently, when Christianity was suppressed in Japan, exclusively on the

30. Settlement on the Menam, which Kaempfer ascended as far as Ayutthaya. The sketch was engraved for the *History of Japan* (vol.1, pl.III).

31. Siamese boat and temple. These designs were also included, though altered in form, in the *History of Japan* (vol.1, pl.I, III).

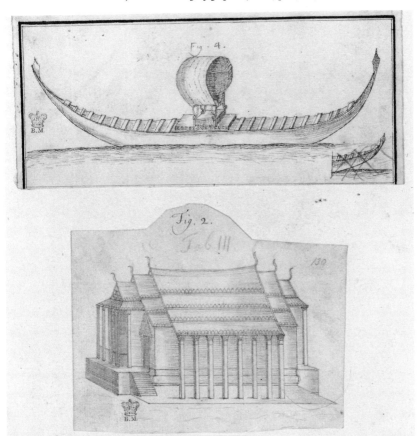

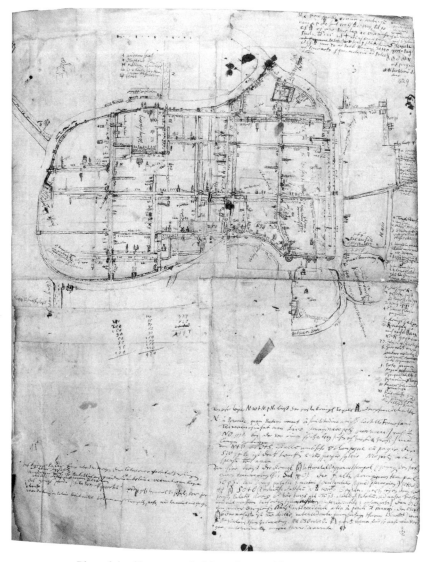

32. Plan of the Siamese capital Ayutthaya, with commentary by Kaempfer and measurements that show how accurately he worked despite the shortage of time.

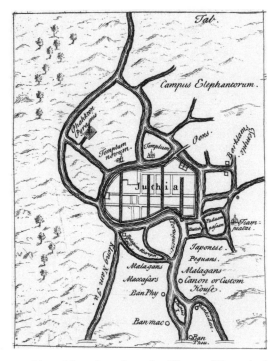

33. Plan of Ayutthaya from the *History of Japan* (vol. 1, pl. VII).

development of trade.[2] The strange island state also attracted constant attention from botanists[3] and cultural geographers.[4] Apart from its character as part of the exotic East, its seclusion from the external world in 1637 had made it even more attractive, especially as the trading profits of the Dutch were still rewarding despite all the restrictions.[5]

On 7 May 1690[6] Kaempfer embarked on the *Waelstroom*, one of the ships that sailed on a regular circuit from Batavia to east Asia. Having coasted along Sumatra and the Malay Peninsula, she entered the Gulf of Siam and on 6 June reached the estuary of the Menam, where the Company's factory lay. Kaempfer immediately attempted to botanise, though without much success. He travelled about a hundred kilometres up the Menam in a lighter, reaching Ayutthaya, the capital of the kingdom of Siam, on the morning of 11 June.

Of the activities of the Dutchmen Kaempfer reports primarily that an audience took place with the 'Berklam', the chancellor of the Siamese kingdom.

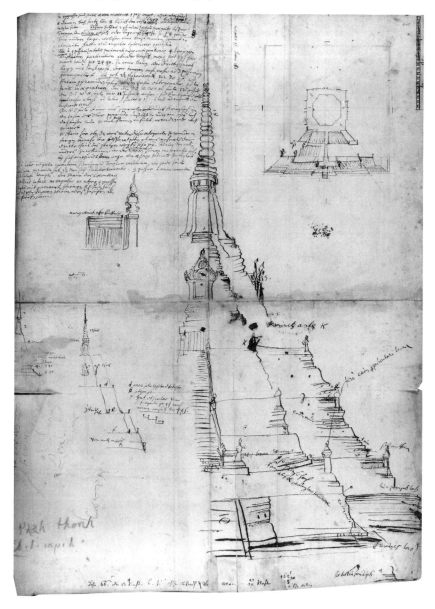

34. Sketches of the Puka 'thon at Ayutthaya, with measurements. This example also demonstrates the precision of Kaempfer's observations.

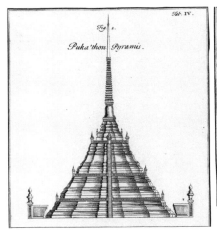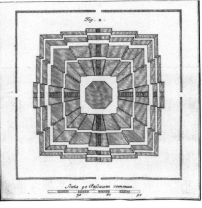

35. Puka 'thon. Engravings from the *History of Japan*, vol.1, pl.IV.

Despite the fact that he probably did not have much spare time, the amount of information that he gathered during the bare month that he spent in Thailand is astonishing. It should be remembered, moreover, that he can hardly have prepared himself for Thailand. The chapter entitled 'The present condition of the Siamese court', with its description of the capital, occupies all of 29 pages in Dohm's edition of his work on Japan, added to which there are a number of illustrations. Despite the brevity of the notes on Thailand, they are by no means unimportant, for again Kaempfer succeeds in presenting the quintessence of all aspects – history, cultural geography, architecture, language, religion and other matters – so that his exposition remains significant for Thai studies to this day. This is especially true if one reads the notes he made on the spot and not merely the finished manuscript, 'Present-day Japan', which forms the basis for Scheuchzer's English translation, and that in turn for Dohm's re-translation into German.[7] However, it also reveals the points on which Kaempfer was mistaken or drew the wrong conclusions.

On 4 July the Dutchmen left Ayutthaya, adverse weather on the Menam preventing Kaempfer from making any further observations on the nature of the river. Having shipped a new cargo on board the *Waelstroom*, the master weighed anchor on 11 July. After rounding Cambodia and South Vietnam he set a course to the north-west, leaving the Gulf of Tonkin to port. The voyage was slow and arduous, as the navigation required special care owing to the ubiquitous shallows and semi-submerged

36. Willem van Outhoorn (1635-1720), Governor General of the Dutch East India Company 1691-1704. From: F. W. Stapel, *De Gouverneurs-Generaal van Nederlandsch Indië in beeld en woord*. Den Haag, 1941.

rocks. With the Formosa Strait behind them, the course was set further east towards Japan. On 25 August a storm blew up which raged with few intermissions until 11 September, causing considerable damage to the ship and her cargo. Kaempfer also complains that his baggage, including a large number of manuscripts, had been damaged by salt water. On 22 September the ship reached Goto island opposite the bay of Nagasaki and around midnight on the 23rd the entrance to the bay itself, but could not pass the latter during the night because of dangerous rocks. At 10 o'clock in the morning she arrived at a point half a nautical mile off Nagasaki and dropped her night anchor. The following day was taken up with the well-known Japanese procedure of checking the newly arrived ship and questioning the crew. The names of all the foreigners were listed, while the cargo was registered and parts of it were sealed.

On the historical background to the policy of seclusion (*sakoku*) only the following needs to be said. After the initial positive Japanese-European contacts during the sixteenth century, conflicts nevertheless developed as the European missionary orders attempted to extend their influence. When various measures adopted by the shoguns failed to achieve lasting results, all Europeans were expelled from the country in 1637, above all the Christian missionaries and the Portuguese who had collaborated closely with them. Following that, only the Dutch succeeded in obtaining permission to trade, at the price of absolute control. Their factory was established in 1641 on the artificially constructed island of Deshima off Nagasaki. Until the opening up of Japan in the nineteenth century Deshima remained the only place of entry for Europeans into Japan.[8]

Kaempfer himself disembarked on 26 September 1690: 'I [transferred] with all my belongings to Deshima, where I moved into the house that had been allocated to me.'[9] Thus began an adventure, the nature of which Kaempfer could scarcely have imagined.

7. *Kaempfer's stay at Deshima and his journeys to Edo*

A mere account of Kaempfer's experiences in Japan and an analysis of the material he gathered there could by themselves easily fill a book. He has rightly always been included among those travellers who, given the circumstances, contributed an extraordinary amount towards knowledge of Japan during the eighteenth and early nineteenth centuries. For this reason he will always be regarded as one of the 'Japanese classics' in a European language. In this connection one should not forget the writings on Japan by the Jesuits, who established the thematic catalogue for descriptions of Japan with their dispatches, annual reports and 'histories' and who laid much of the groundwork for the following period.

Kaempfer was of course not the first European to write extensively about Japan. Despite its almost total isolation Europeans were repeatedly able to gather information and bring it out of Japan.[1] The reports, written by people of very different educational backgrounds, vary considerably with regard to their information value. There are accounts by travellers who spent long periods in Japan[2] as well as more extensive special studies[3] and brief sketches.[4] Even travellers who only touched at Japan during one stage of their 'East India' voyage used that as an occasion to record their impressions.[5] There was also the regional geography of Varenius in which, although he had never been in Japan himself, he drew on a number of authorities on Japan and geographers to compile an account of Nippon.[6]

At least a brief reference should be made here to Arnold Montanus' *Gedenkwaerdige gesantschappen der Oost-Indische Maatschappij in 't Vereenigde Nederland, aan de kaisaren van Japan* (Amsterdam, 1669) and to Christian Arnold's collection *Wahrhaftige Beschreibungen dreyer mächtiger Königreiche Japan, Siam und Corea [...]* (Nuremberg, 1672). The latter work contains a number of texts on Japan by, among others, Caron, Hagenaer, Martin, Schouten and Hamel Wurfbäin. With all their shortcomings, the above-mentioned books constituted a large storehouse of knowledge for European readers.

Even before Kaempfer's sojourn in Japan there was thus already a fairly extensive body of literature on Japan.[7] But did it really enable the reader to gain an accurate impression of the specific characteristics of Japanese culture and daily life? Most readers were probably satisfied with highlights of information.[8] Even the more extended accounts, however, were often constrained by certain stereotypes. Under those conditions Kaempfer's work on Japan was to become a success, as he was the first to '[blend] his own experiences and researches with the older literature into a comprehensive description of a paradigmatic quality'.[9]

In his capacity as the Dutch East India Company's physician at Deshima, Kaempfer had the advantage of coming into contact with many Japanese. Their desire to learn about European medicine led them to adopt a relatively open attitude.[10]

Having rapidly surveyed the situation, Kaempfer soon adapted himself to the new possibilities and conditions of working. In the preface to his *Geschichte und Beschreibung von Japan* Kaempfer describes his analysis of the situation at that time and his reaction: 'But as we Dutchmen are only merchants, who in Japan have the lowest and most despised status, and as we are moreover regarded among them as suspect guests and always live in custody, one has to adjust one's entire conduct to flattering and satisfying the pride and self-interest of the Japanese and to show oneself agreeable and obliging to their wishes if one wants to win favour with such a proud people and obtain anything from them. I employed these means

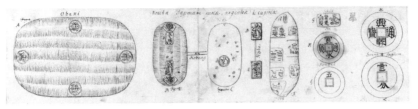

37. Japanese coins of copper and gold. This drawing provided the pattern for the engraving in the *History of Japan*, vol.2, pl.XIX. In the centre is a 'kobang', the gold coin on which Japanese-Dutch trade was based (the kobang trade).

and thereby gained the confidence of our superiors and interpreters. These people made daily visits to the residence of our nation, Deshima, and in particular to my house, and I managed to establish a closer relationship with them, I believe, than any other European can boast of since our present long-standing trading arrangements were established.'[11] Kaempfer, in turn, gave them all the information they wanted about 'medical science', astronomy and mathematics and listened to his interlocutors with the 'cordial' assistance of 'European liqueurs': 'This made them so friendly towards me that I was able to enquire with the greatest possible freedom, in detail and circumstantially, about their natural, spiritual and temporal history and anything else I wished to know. No one refused to give me information to the best of his knowledge, even concerning the most forbidden matters, provided I was alone with him.'[12]

He received considerable help from an 'educated youth' who, in the guise of a servant, was really set to spy on him.[13] Their mutual sympathy obviously outweighed this, however. Indeed the circumstance favoured Kaempfer, for in Imamura Gen'emon Eisei (1671-1736) he found a person who, as a member of a family of interpreters, understood his concerns and helped to promote the intercultural dialogue by gathering information. He assisted him in procuring material as far as he could – thus putting himself in danger of being exposed as a spy and executed. Apart from his contact with Kaempfer, it is interesting to note that he was one of the most prominent interpreters at Deshima at the turn of the eighteenth century and played the leading role in that regard in Dutch-Japanese relations for almost forty years. Many a Dutch chief merchant described him as the 'hub, around which everything turns'.

In his book Kaempfer concerns himself with every aspect of Japan that

was accessible to him – although that excludes the visual arts and literature as well as the mathematical sciences. He gives a detailed description
of the geographical position of the islands, their climate and the flora
and fauna. He discusses at length the origin of the Japanese people and
provides extensive extracts from the Japanese annals. He also deals
thoroughly, if not as the first European, with Confucianism and the
'various religious and philosophical sects'.[14]

Kaempfer had already included a chapter on Japan's policy of isolation
(*sakoku*) in the *Amoenitates exoticae*.[15] Dohm rightly incorporated it, for
thematic reasons, in his edition of the work on Japan[16] and added a commentary to it. In short, for a variety of reasons Kaempfer comes down in
favour of the *sakoku*: Japan was predestined by its island nature to be isolated and had successfully warded off foreign invasions. Despite certain
deficiencies, Japan possessed an advanced culture of which Kaempfer
had only a rudimentary knowledge (he knew nothing, for instance, of
Japanese mathematics or literature). Its weakening by the penetration
of foreign customs and, finally, the aggressive Christian mission had
justified the policy. This standpoint, at which Kaempfer arrived simply
from his own observations and a reading of the sources, enabled him to
move ahead of his time. He tried not to see the history of other countries
in a preconceived manner through European eyes but to understand the
motive forces within their cultures from the other side.[17]

It is only natural that Kaempfer, who was almost entirely dependent
on Japanese informants, arrived at the wrong conclusions in certain
respects.[18] In this he very much resembles Olearius, who did attempt to
correct misconceptions in his account of Persia but was himself in no
position to assess correctly all aspects of its exotic culture.[19] Nevertheless,
Kaempfer's historical chapters should not be underrated, as they provided the most detailed source of information on Japanese conditions
available in Europe for a long time, surpassed only by Schamberger's
observations.[20]

However, the aspect of Kaempfer's work that still makes it so important even today is the account of his two journeys to Edo (Tokyo) to the
residence of the ruling shogun, who in Kaempfer's time was Tokugawa
Tsunayoshi. The Dutch were obliged to undertake this journey once a
year. On their part they presented gifts as an act of homage for the permission to trade from Deshima, while the conditions of trade and prices
were settled again anew on the occasion of each such visit. Only a few
Europeans before Kaempfer, and none after him until Thunberg and

38. The retinue of the Dutch mission to Edo (Tokyo). The numerals refer
to legends on the back of the drawing describing the various individuals
and their roles; no.15 reads: 'A Dutch surgeon and a valet' – in other
words, Kaempfer himself. In depicting the procession Kaempfer draws
on the model of an extended file current in the seventeenth century. The
drawing provided the pattern for the engraving in the *History of Japan*,
vol.2, pl.XXII.

Siebold, had the opportunity to observe Japanese life so closely in this
way.

After the complex preparations and arrangements, Kaempfer describes
the condition of the roads, the manner of travelling and forms of accom-
modation, the topographical guides and the customs of travellers from
different social strata, and not least the expenses incurred by the Dutch
in this annual enterprise. He suggests the following reasons for the extent
of travelling by the Japanese: 'The highways of the country are daily filled
with an incredible number of people and are in certain seasons as crowded
as the streets in a populous European city; I can vouch for that from my
own experience on the Tokaido, which is unquestionably the greatest of
the seven main routes, as I have passed along it four times. The reasons
for this are partly the large number of inhabitants of the kingdom, partly
the numerous journeys they undertake, contrary to the custom of other
nations.'[21] Further on he deals extensively with the various types of pil-
grims and beggars and finally with the other travellers along the trunk

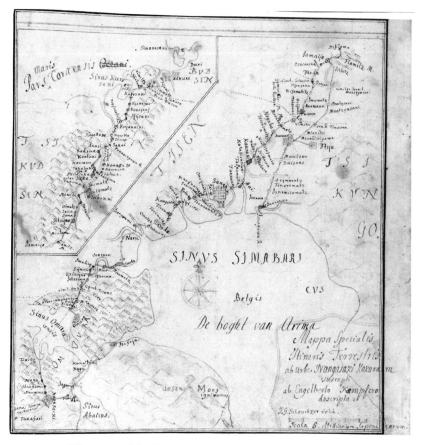

39. The route of the Dutch to Edo, here the section from Nagasaki to
Shimonoseki. It should be emphasised that the route maps are not drawn
by Kaempfer but that the author is J. G. Scheuchzer; however,
Kaempfer's maps served as his models.

roads: 'The busy throng on our road is also substantially increased by the
petty traders and peasant children who run about until nightfall offering
the travellers their paltry wares, which include cakes, in which the sugar
is scarcely perceptible, pastry, "soccani" and various kinds of roots boiled
in water, printed route guides or travel handbooks, straw shoes for people
and horses, ropes and cords, toothpicks and other trifles made, according
to the local environment, from straw, reeds, bamboo or wood. Likewise,
in many places in or near villages stand parties of bearers with "cangos"
or sedan chairs, as well as servants holding carelessly and badly saddled

horses which they offer the weary foot-traveller as far as the next post-house or wherever they wish to go, for a small fee.'[22]

The 'curious' Kaempfer resorted to a ruse in order to obtain a more exact and lasting record of his route. He hid a compass, which he secretly took with him, in a bark box, passed it off as writing equipment and then always pretended that he wished to identify the plants that were handed to him and to write notes about them.[23] As he was known to be a physician and a botanist, this method worked extremely well and at the end of the journey even earned him special praise from the Japanese authorities in Nagasaki for his devotion to botany, which was held in particularly high regard by the Japanese.

On 13 February 1691[24] the large mission set out from Deshima.[25] It travelled from Nagasaki to Kokura, crossed over to Shimonoseki and embarked there on two small vessels in which it sailed north-east across the inland sea to Osaka. An audience was held there with the governor. The Dutchmen covered the distance from Osaka to Miyako (Kyoto), the imperial city, in one long day's journey. After staying there for two days, they continued. It took them eleven days (2-13 March) to travel the remaining distance to Edo (Tokyo), which they accomplished along the Tokaido, the 'Eastern Sea Road', mostly beside or near the coast. The mission had required 29 days to cover the entire distance. Its sojourn in the city lasted three weeks (22 days), a period that was filled with a great variety of visits, audiences and the presentation of the gifts. The really important ceremony, in which the current chief merchant paid his respects to the shogun,[26] consisted simply of his crawling towards the shogun, who was seated among the 'councillors of the realm', bowing his head and crawling away backwards. This took place after hours of waiting and the ceremonious deposition of the gifts, and it is understandable that Kaempfer's comment is mildly critical: 'That is all there was to the entire brief ceremony during an audience for which the preparations had been elaborate.'[27]

Another reception followed, namely before the ladies of the court together with the shogun.[28] The captain of the Dutchmen, von Buitenhem, expresses his gratitude for the favour shown in permitting the Dutch to trade with the Japanese. But then comes what Kaempfer calls 'real clowning': the participants in the audience have to walk about, dance, jump, imitate a drunk, paint, read in Dutch and German, sing, etc., all in the European manner. Kaempfer, whose musical talent also earned him an appearance, sang a 'German love song':[29]

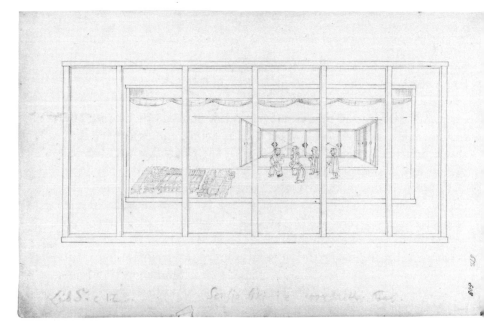

40. Audience chamber in the palace of the Shogun in Edo. The figures indicate the spatial proportions.

41. Audience chamber in the *History of Japan*, vol.2, pl.XXXI. Even if the engraving differs from and is less vivid than the drawing, it does present to the European reader an interior of which there were no previous representations in the West.

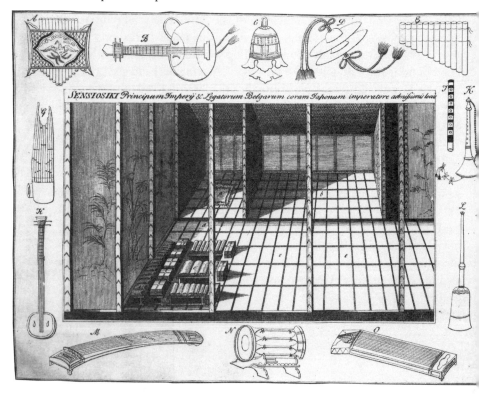

I my duty do recall
On this far-flung foreign shore,
Fairest whom I see no more,
    You who hold my heart in thrall,
Whom I once did swear an oath
    In good faith, with honour due,
By the Light that guides us both,
    To remain for ever true.

    But why speak of debt or duty?
What's a promise or a vow?
That which Heaven does allow
    As a gift divine – Your beauty,
And such virtue as is found
    Nowhere that the sky enfolds,
Is the chain by which I'm bound,
    Is the prison that me holds.

    And to worsen yet my plight
I, poor wretch, my mind did set
You, dear Angel, to forget
    By such far and headlong flight.
Mountains, savage lands uncharted,
    Noble rivers of great fame
Cannot keep me from you parted
    Nor will quench my burning flame.

    Oh great Emperor, Heaven's Son,
Master of these distant lands,
Rich in tribute, strong in hands,
    Of your wealth I will have none
But declare that in my mind
    All your splendour, gleaming gold,
Ladies painted and refined
    To my Angel nought I hold.

    Take your court and its effeteness,
Take this land and all its treasure,
Here on earth my only pleasure
    Is the charming, modest sweetness
That my Florimene displays,
    She who still my heart does stir,
We who long through all our days,
    She for me and I for her.[30]

This ballad is entirely in the tradition of the German love song. Kaempfer uses familiar literary formulas, such as the opposition between distance and proximity or the modest natural beauty of the beloved contrasted with the artificiality of other women. If there is any reference to his personal life it is highly stylised. One should remember that at the time of the performance, if one includes the period of his schooling away from home, Kaempfer had already lived a wandering life for 24 years.[31]

It is hardly surprising that Kaempfer's description of Edo is not very detailed, as his days were so busy – at least by his own account – that he had no time left over to take a close look at the town and draw a plan of it. However, he managed to overcome that disadvantage to some extent by acquiring a street map of Edo. It is the latter that forms the basis of the plan in the editions of Scheuchzer and Dohm.[32]

On 5 April 1691 the mission left Edo to make its way back by the same route (apart from a few minor detours), and on 8 May it returned to Deshima again.

The second journey to the court in Edo, which lasted from 2 March until 12 May 1692, must again have provided welcome relief from the daily monotony at Deshima both for Kaempfer and for the other members of the mission. Apart from his geographical introduction, Kaempfer describes so many events and localities that it would require a detailed commentary to do justice to his account. Nonetheless, in order to provide a general account of his achievement, his work on Japan will be summarised below by subject areas and the results of his researches outlined. The aspects covered are medicine, botany, cartography and, finally, the description of the land and its inhabitants.

The relationship between Japanese and Europeans, as far as medicine is concerned, can be viewed from two aspects: on the one hand the Europeans became acquainted with a medical science that was unknown to them, while they on the other hand also provided their hosts with new information. By describing therapeutic methods Kaempfer himself contributed something to the dissemination of western medical knowledge in Japan, though he did not, like some of his famous successors, help to create a new approach to the subject. In this field he concentrated primarily on two methods, namely acupuncture and moxibustion, although both of these were known in Europe before his time.[33] The medical science that evolved in Europe during the seventeenth and eighteenth centuries was hardly accommodating to either of these methods. Although Galen had been surpassed and some progress had been made in both the theory and practice of anatomy and physiology, the field was still dominated by the numerous spa physicians and barber-surgeons, most of whom practised without much medical knowledge. Under those circum-

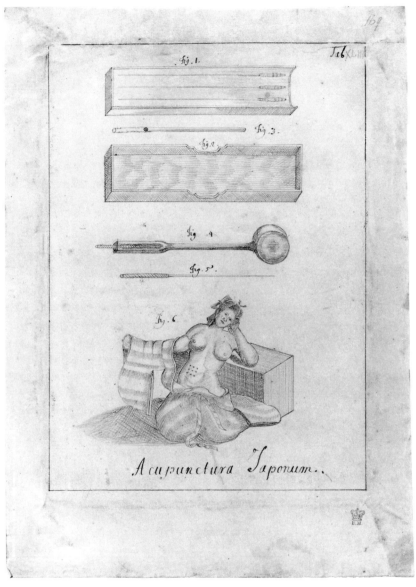

42. 'Acupunctura Japonum'. The drawing shows a number of needles in a
small case, a little hammer and a needle for 'needle-tapping' and a
diagram of acupuncture points. There are various acupuncture needles
and small cases listed in Sloane's acquisition inventory, but some of them
seem to have been lost.

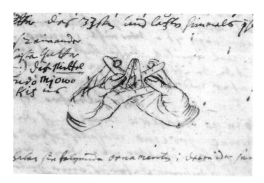

43. Mudra, finger positions for magical practices. Kaempfer recorded these in detail but did not include them in his manuscript 'Heutiges Japan'.

stances it was only natural that neither the account of the theoretical principles of acupuncture by Cleyer nor that of its practical application by De Bondt, ten Rhijne and Kaempfer found a particularly receptive audience.

Yet Kaempfer's description of acupuncture and moxibustion (which was reprinted in his work on Japan in the same form in which it had been included in the *Amoenitates exoticae*) was one of the few authentic contributions on the subject. Kaempfer describes exactly what the acupuncture instruments looked like, how the needles were placed and for which disorders – mainly colics – they were used. However, it becomes clear from his account, as well as those of his predecessors Cleyer and ten Rhijne, that there was no consensus among the Asians themselves about the application of these methods: 'as each follows either his own or his teacher's experience, always emphasising one part rather than another, there is scarcely a single part of the entire body that should not be singed, according to the various opinions.'[34]

In the case of moxibustion a half-inch long wad of the finest fibres of the *Artemisia vulgaris* (mugwort) was set alight on the spot where the pain was felt and was allowed to burn down to the skin. This method also specified particular areas of the body that should be treated for corresponding diseases. Kaempfer gives a detailed account of the rules by which this had to be done and names 14 areas (probably only a small selection of all the possible ones) that may be singed. For demonstration purposes he adds a diagram that purports to show all the 'focal points'.[35] Yet this also reveals the limits imposed on him by his presumably fairly restricted knowledge of the language: the design, copied from a Japanese

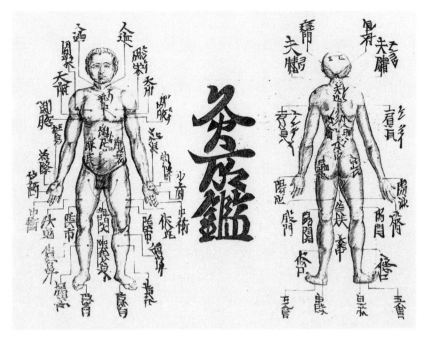

44. Moxibustion diagram from the *Amoenitates exoticae*, p.601. No
pattern for this engraving has so far been traced; the figure does not show
the points that should be singed but those where singeing ought to be
avoided.

prototype, does not in fact show the focal points but, on the contrary,
those which should preferably not be singed or were taboo.[36]

For his time, Kaempfer shows an astonishing lack of bias towards the
alien methods of cure and treatment. It was not only his contemporaries
who mentally resisted the exotic methods and practices; even the enlightened Dohm had problems with Kaempfer's attempt to approach
Japanese attitudes and thought processes in an unbiassed way.[37] It is worth
mentioning, however, though it cannot be discussed in detail here, that
the various medical practices were indeed subjected to thorough analysis
and intensive correspondence in professional circles. The dissemination
of such information in Europe began as early as the sixteenth century,
though it may well not have been generally known in the medical world.[38]

In Europe, as in Japan, botany was closely associated with medicine, as
the extraction of medicinal drugs depended on a knowledge of the herbs
from which they were extracted. As the Japanese were equally interested

45. Japanese plant called 'faadsi'; in the *Amoenitates exoticae*, pp.794-6: 'Fási no ki. Arbor vernicifera spuria, sylvestris, angustifolia.' A lacquer tree, the berries of which produce a tallow suitable for candle-making. Unfortunately Kaempfer never fulfilled his intention of publishing a 'Herbarium transgangeticum'. The few engravings of plants included in the fifth section of the *Amoenitates* represent only a minute selection from hundreds of magnificent drawings.

in their native flora, they understood Kaempfer's desire to see unknown and rare plants and willingly assisted him, for instance during his journey to Edo. The fifth chapter of his *Amoenitates exoticae* contains this Japanese flora, listing all the plants that he had been able to find during his first journey in 1691. Although his aim in this survey was completeness, he nevertheless omitted those plants for which he could establish neither the name nor the written character. He described 420 plants – far more than Cleyer and Meister before him. Although he was able to include only 28 drawings in the *Amoenitates*, he brought home with him in all hundreds of drawings, intending to publish them as a 'Herbarium transgangeticum'.[39]

It is not only the number of new discoveries that he made in this field that is significant, however, but also his ability to describe them. Through his drawings the plants even today confront the viewer as if they were still growing, and they often seem to burst off the page with the vitality of their vegetable forms.[40] If one recalls how difficult it was until the nineteenth century to produce effective medicinal drugs, it is easier to appreciate Kaempfer's efforts. By assembling a large collection of plants and describing it accurately he would be able to prepare the way for important work. The same was done by other botanists and physicians of his period when they communicated their discoveries in Asia to colleagues in Europe, either directly by letters and 'circulars' or through the learned societies. Among those who belong in this category are Cleyer, ten Rhijne and Scheffer.[41]

However, Kaempfer's work on Japan had a decisive effect on later generations owing to the fact that he was the first to provide a really clear description of the interior of the country and not merely a rough indication of it. It is the above-mentioned route maps that gave the eighteenth-century reader an impression of south-eastern Honshu of a previously unparalleled accuracy. Quite apart from the personal achievement, they constitute a milestone in the European mapping of Japan. Even the doyen of Japanese cartography, Count Teleki, had a wholly positive opinion of them: 'On the whole, Kaempfer deserves high praise for these maps, considering the rough and not over-scrupulous methods he had to employ under the restrictions imposed by the suspicious Japanese. With regard to the orientation and distances and in general everything derived from personal observation, they are the best to have been drawn until then.'[42] The entire route of the journey is recorded on four plates containing new sectional maps. These sheets, which may at first

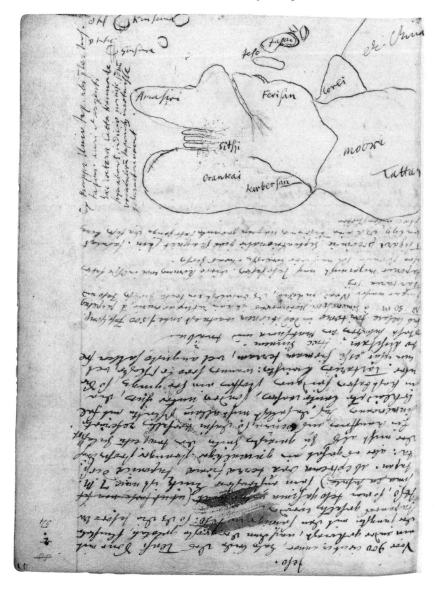

46. Japan and the mainland of China with Siberia. The cartography of
this region had by no means been elucidated in Kaempfer's time and,
due to the lack of sources, he himself failed to arrive at an accurate
representation of Japan. His map of Japan in the *History of Japan* exactly
reflects that state of knowledge (vol.1, pl.VIII).

sight appear rather plain, in reality represent a high point in the history of travel. In the first place, as Teleki rightly pointed out, they provide an image of southern and south-eastern Japan with an amount of detail never previously seen and which would only be exceeded during the nineteenth century. However, as Kaempfer's work is not an atlas but a travel account and cultural geography, the information content of the maps is decisively enhanced by the text, which provides a very precise record of the journey. In other words, Kaempfer's detailed description of the route adds relief and vitality to the visual representation, while on the other hand the map identifies the localities referred to in the text and, by relating the latter to a specific geographical point, gives it that immediacy which provided the most stimulating ingredient of true (as well as fictional!) travel narratives in the eighteenth century. In the interplay between map and text Kaempfer produces an image that transcends the external form of the landscape and surpasses other creations of this kind by its precision and liveliness.

His general map of Japan also influenced later ones. Following the earliest representations of the Japanese islands in European atlases[43] during the last quarter of the sixteenth century, all of which were still far removed from the true shape of the island realm, the Portuguese Teixeira in 1595 created an image that was to remain influential until the middle of the seventeenth century. All the leading cartographers, such as Mercator, Hondius and Jansson, followed his model for want of better information. It was only with the map of the Jesuit Philippe Briet in 1650, and above all with the one produced five years later by Martinus Martini, a member of the same order, that a stage of visualisation was reached that approached far more closely to the true geographical facts. The problem of representing north-eastern Japan was, of course, still resolved in a most unsatisfactory way, while the other regions also displayed a number of inaccuracies owing to the Japanese policy of secrecy. However, the isolation of the country was not complete enough to prevent Japanese cartographic materials from finding their way to Europe[44] – as indeed Kaempfer himself smuggled town plans and maps out of Japan.[45] Although his general outline of the Japanese islands does not differ from that of other contemporary maps[46] it already, together with the map of Reland, represents an advance on earlier ones in its internal subdivision; the external shape, however, is definitely retrogressive compared to that of Martinus Martini (Atlas Sinensis, 1655). It was nevertheless his map which, following its publication by Scheuchzer in 1727, was to exert an influence throughout the eighteenth century.[47]

It is also the element of 'personal observation', as Teleki says, that makes his description of the country and its people so enjoyable not only for the specialists but also to a wider circle of readers even at the end of the eighteenth century. The words 'history' and 'account' in the title given to it by Dohm are not Kaempfer's own, however. He entitled his manuscript 'Present-day Japan. On two journeys to the court, experienced and described, etc.' That is a much more accurate description of his aims, whereas the all-embracing approach suggested by the later editor is not yet present. He wants to convey to the reader the Japan which he himself had experienced. That he was nevertheless aware of the underlying historical dimension is shown, for example, by his extracts from the Japanese annals and by his account of the 'various religious parties in the Japanese realm', whose characteristics he attempts to grasp from the perspective of their historical evolution. (In so doing, he is the first to provide a detailed description of Shintoism.)

The attention to detail and the vividness with which he presents his account to the reader explains why it was still highly regarded in the nineteenth century. For those reasons, and especially because it does not deal with a familiar and accessible region, the topographical survey produces a graphic image of one of the oldest cultural landscapes on earth. His procedure is straightforward. Kaempfer takes the opportunity, on every possible occasion, to combine his description of the natural features with an account of Japanese culture. Particular temples and houses, as well as strange customs and practices, peculiar individuals whom he happened to encounter – all of these attract his attention. Yet his account is not restricted to the unusual and the curious but, on the contrary, extends to the everyday life that he is able to observe in all its motley variety outside Deshima. All social strata are brought into his field of vision, from the prostitutes to the people of rank, from beggars and monks to the dignitaries of state – he tries to describe them all faithfully in words. It is these numerous details that make his work so graphic and, above all, makes the object of his exertions more comprehensible than in earlier accounts.

8. *Homeward voyage from Asia*

Kaempfer must have asked himself what his life would be like when he returned from Japan. The reports he had heard of the unfavourable conditions in Europe at first dampened his enthusiasm for returning there.[1] He expressed himself rather dolefully in a letter to his brother Joachim, probably at the end of 1690: 'I have no plans to see any more in the East, apart from a few places, but as I feel somewhat weakened by my years and manifold labours I now desire no more *quam in angulo alicujus oppiduli requiescere posse* and there devote the rest of my life to worshipping and thanking my God, who has so wondrously preserved me and whom I can but serve *tacito animo*. Therefore, God willing, I am ready to come back next year with the returning ships, unless perilous conditions in Europe or the advice so seriously proffered by my dearly beloved brother or a violent *fatum* should prevent me.'[2] In addition he writes to Andreas Cleyer regarding a commission: he would preferably, 'God willing, bring it over personally next year; since there are no homebound ships in the region I am obliged to remain here for another year.'[3] There was thus no question of his 'preferring to continue his fruitful researches in Japan'.[4] In fact, as soon as he arrived at Deshima he wished he were back in Batavia 'in order to be on hand for the return voyage to the fatherland; especially as I hope to have the good fortune to travel there under the gracious protection of my patron Mr.Lycochthon.'[5]

In August 1692 four ships arrived at Batavia, three of them sailing onward on 25, 26 and 27 October. Kaempfer left Japan on the flag-ship *Pampus* on the 30th of the same month. And now the moment arrives when he brings to safety the material that he has collected in Japan so assiduously and under such hazardous conditions; in his work on Japan he writes laconically: 'I now retrieved my Japanese things, both printed and handwritten, which I had secretly hidden and distributed among the cargoes of those ships.'[6] These brief words display his shrewdness but also, above all, the danger involved in his smuggling of the extensive notes and materials out of Japan.

Information regarding the following months is scarce. As Kaempfer could not expect any support from the Dutch East India Company in

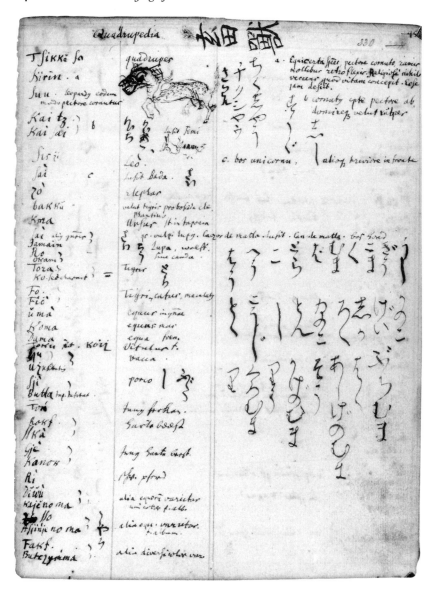

47. Kaempfer's notes on the Japanese names of various animals, showing his efforts to learn the language. The characters were probably written out by a Japanese rather than by Kaempfer himself. There were certainly Dutchmen in the seventeenth century who spoke Japanese better than he, but only Kaempfer recorded his observations, 'with depressing diligence' (Michel), thereby providing us with precise information about the linguistic situation in his time.

Batavia his best option was to return home. He merely attempted to obtain the salary for 20 months and eleven days that was still due to him from Persia, as well as his expenses of 300 rix-dollars for medicines.[7] Perhaps for reasons of economy he returned to the Netherlands, again on the *Pampus*, not as a passenger but as *boekhouder*, in other words as the ship's book-keeper, on a salary of 45 guilders.[8]

The *Pampus* sailed straight across the Indian Ocean to southern Africa. After a few pleasant months at the Cape – during which he was almost persuaded to stay[9] – and a stormy passage from there, the *Pampus* berthed at Amsterdam on 6 October 1693. He now stood on European soil again after living abroad for ten and a half years. Including his years at boarding schools, however, Kaempfer had by then been away from home for about 26 years, a considerable length of time in the life of a person during the second half of the seventeenth century, bearing in mind that most people still lived out their lives within a radius of a few kilometres.

9. *Conferment of doctorate and return to Lemgo*

One of the reasons why Kaempfer decided to return to Europe was undoubtedly that he wished to complete his studies, which were still unfinished, by gaining a qualification that would enable him to pursue a secure professional career at home.[1]

Initially he stayed in Amsterdam as a guest of Johann Parvé, whom he had come to know in his role as financial secretary in Batavia. They must have developed a strong mutual sympathy, though they had only spent a short time together in south-east Asia. Here Kaempfer also met again one of his few patrons, Wibrand Lycochthon. As early as 21 November 1693 he registered in the medical faculty of the National University in Leiden. Only a few days later, on 24 November, he underwent the 'secret' examinations which he had to pass in order to enter the public examination, the *rigorosum*. Simultaneously, with the assistance of his friend Wilhelm Hovius, he revised the dissertation that he had written during his return voyage from Asia, 'that premature birth, brought into the world at sea,' as he wrote to Hovius, who corrected it.[2]

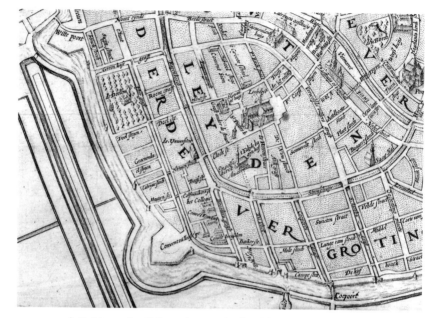

48. Leiden – detail from the map in *Les délices de Leiden [...]*, Leiden, 1712. The 'Nonnensteech', where Kaempfer resided 1693-94, runs close by the University.

The dissertation, entitled *Disputatio medica inauguralis exhibens decadem observationum exoticarum [...]*, covers ten phenomena of natural science and medicine which he had observed in the course of his travels. He deals with 'Scythian lamb', the acridity of the Caspian Sea, Persian mummy, the electric ray of the Persian Gulf, dragon's blood resin, the Medina worm (Dracunculus), hydrocele and Madura foot as well as acupuncture and moxibustion.

Summarising the observations made by Kaempfer, the following picture emerges. Despite a few obvious errors, attributable to the limited medical and microbiological knowledge and methods of his time,[3] he describes a number of phenomena not previously known in that form or at that level of detail. These include the chapters on the electric ray,[4] dragon's blood resin, the Medina worm, hydrocele and Madura foot.[5] His accounts of acupuncture and moxibustion were not, strictly speaking, new to the medical profession. However, Kaempfer's reports are an important stage in the history of the dissemination of these practices in Europe, not only because they are among the earliest descriptions but also because of

DISPUTATIO MEDICA
INAUGURALIS
Exhibens
DECADEM
OBSERVATIONUM
EXOTICARUM
QVAM
FAVENTE DIVINA GRATIA,
Ex Auctoritate Magnifici D. Rectoris
D. CAROLI DRELINCURTII,
Regii olim in Galliis Medici, nunc verò in hac
Univerſitate Profeſſorum Antiquiſſimi,
NEC NON
Ampliſſimi Senatus Academici Conſenſu , & Alma
Facultatis MEDICÆ *Decreto*,
PRO GRADU DOCTORATUS,
Summiſque in ▓▓▓▓ MEDICINA Honoribus & Privilegiis
rite ac legitime conſequendis,
Publico examini ſubjicit
ENGELBERT KEMPFER, L. L. Weſtph.
Ad diem 22. *Aprilis, horá locòque ſolitis.*

LUGDUNI BATAVORUM,
Apud ABRAHAMUM ELZEVIER,
Academiæ Typographum. M D C XC IV.

49. Title-page of Kaempfer's medical dissertation from 1694, which he
wrote during his return voyage to Europe and submitted in Leiden.

50. Nicolaas Witsen. Portrait from 1677. After his return from Asia
Kaempfer apparently tried with his assistance to find employment in the
Netherlands.

his endeavour to achieve exactness and remove obscurities, such as the lack of precise instructions on cauterising.[6] In his edition of the work on Japan Dohm rightly included the chapters on Japanese therapeutic methods from the *Amoenitates*.[7]

The *rigorosum* took place on 22 April 1694. With the renowned Professor Charles Drelincourt presiding, Kaempfer was examined by the practising physician Frederik Dekkers, the anatomist Govard Bidloo and his thesis supervisor Paulus Hermann – a widely travelled scholar, well versed in botany – and a doctorate was conferred on him, '*honoribus et privilegiis*', with great ceremony and solemnity.[8]

Kaempfer apparently made an attempt to find employment during his stay in the Netherlands on this occasion. No details of this are recorded, but it is known that he sent a copy of his dissertation to the renowned Nicolaas Witsen.[9] In July he visited Mesdach and Hovius in Rotterdam.[10] However, his efforts to find a patron were unsuccessful. After July 1694 Kaempfer is no longer traceable in the Netherlands; he had left for home.

10. *Last years in Lieme*

After his return from the Netherlands Kaempfer moved into the Steinhof in Lieme bei Lemgo, which his father had acquired.[1] He planned to work up the material that he had gathered in Asia and to publish it in an expanded form, complemented with the results of research by other scholars. At the same time he practised as a physician in order to earn a living. Then on 7 December 1698 he became physician in ordinary to Friedrich Adolf, Count of Lippe.[2] In addition to his medical practice, however, there was not only his service with the local ruler but also strains of a different kind. In the first place people sought advice and Kaempfer wrote them long letters providing detailed prescriptions.[3]

Added to this was a circumstance that he may not have foreseen but which developed into a major nuisance for him. The word soon got around that there was a doctor living near Lemgo who had resided abroad for many years and had brought back with him a large number of 'curiosities'. And so, if people were in the neighbourhood, they paid a visit to Dr Kaempfer and let him show and explain his treasures to them. He eventually grew tired of these numerous visitors, presumably because

51. Count Friedrich Adolf zur Lippe (reigned 1695-1716), whom Kaempfer served as physician in ordinary.

they always asked the same questions and were reluctant to leave.[4] The visitors included highly placed persons, whom he could not so easily get rid of.[5] As if all that was not enough to make life more difficult for him, there was still worse to come.

On 8 November 1700 Kaempfer wrote to his friend Daniel Parvé: 'At the invitation of others I leave Lippe to visit my relatives, whom I have not seen for years. Now on this trip [...] – induced by the matchmaking

efforts of good friends over meals and by my present situation, I allow myself to be persuaded to marry and put up with the only daughter of a
wealthy merchant, with a very decent dowry, being engaged to me [...]
You ask in surprise why I, in the evening of my life, past the age of forty,
should still take a wife? I might answer you in the words of the comedian:
once in a lifetime one must commit a folly, had I not been led to it by many
weighty considerations, which I will explain to you personally some
time.'[6]

One such reason, for which he unfortunately left no written evidence,
may be regarded as more than a supposition. With the property of his wife
he hoped to free himself from his professional duties in order to be able
to edit his material and prepare it for publication. The period from his
wedding on 18 December 1700 to Maria Sophia Wilstach (1684-1761) to
his death was, on the contrary, to become a 'hell on earth'.

As only Kaempfer's complaints are recorded and nothing but a single
letter from his wife,[7] it is hardly possible to write an account that would
be fair to both sides. The situation, which evolved over a number of years
and in the end probably contributed materially to Kaempfer's physical
and mental decline, was presumably due to the behaviour of both parties.
It becomes apparent from Kaempfer's will that his vexation already began
with the dowry: 'It is also manifest and an incontestable fact that the
dowry which was promised to me in the marriage settlement has up to
the present moment not been duly and fully paid over to me,' writes
Kaempfer in his will.[8] In other words, he appears to have been deceived
about the dowry; other financial benefits were also withheld from him.[9]
His accusations against his wife may be summed up under a few head-
ings: his wife had 'managed the housekeeping badly, much of it left un-
done, neglected, squandered, ruined, frittered away and embezzled from
my share',[10] she had 'often disturbed [him] in *studiis et praxi medica*',[11]
had 'deserted' him[12] and 'entirely refused me my conjugal rights for the
last five years'.[13] The marital discord became so serious that, in the very
last year of his life, Kaempfer addressed a petition to Count Friedrich
Adolf asking him to recommend a divorce.[14]

Yet Kaempfer must also have had some responsibility for the domestic
misery and the breakdown of the marriage. Even if one cannot regard the
relatives of his wife, who naturally took her side,[15] as entirely objective,
their statements do nevertheless make it quite clear that he had not always
treated the young girl in a correct manner.[16] How else can one explain that
the wife of the well-regarded physician Dr Kaempfer demonstrably went

to her parents in Stolzenau an der Weser for two of her three confinements? In 1702 Amalia Florentine (†1705) was baptised in Stolzenau, after 1705 another Amalia (†1714) and in 1710 Friedrich Adolf († after 1715). All the children died from smallpox.

One should also bear in mind that Kaempfer had been away from his homeland not just for more than a decade but, from his time at the school in Hameln until his return from the Netherlands, for about 27 years (discounting his visit to Lemgo before the death of his father). Even if the social outlook formed by the way his father brought him up may still be observed until the very last years of his life,[17] he had completely outgrown the narrow horizons and poverty caused by the economic and political misery of the last few decades in Lemgo. If one recalls, for example, such professionally successful men as Andreas Cleyer or François Caron, of whom there were many in the Middle and Far East, then one realises in what a colourful world Kaempfer had spent a large part of his life. Although he finally sought an escape from his service in the Dutch East India Company, he must have been far too affected by the exoticism of Asia to be able to adjust himself without any problems after his return to the provincial confines of Lemgo.

Moreover, he faced one difficulty after another in editing his work, which he continued to polish and improve. Apart from his disappointment with the inferior engraver Brandshagen, who ruined his illustrations for the *Amoenitates*, he had problems obtaining literature.[18] Some of the books were available in Kaempfer's own library, but he had to acquire many important works through his Dutch friends. That helps to explain why the *Amoenitates exoticae* appeared only in 1712 – eighteen years after his return!

Whereas the letters to Daniel Parvé from the period up to 1705 continually contain requests for books, indicating a phase of intensive work, letters from the following years until the appearance of the *Amoenitates* have evidently not been preserved. Thus nothing is known about the final stage of work on the publication, nor about how Kaempfer reacted to the judgements passed on his book by the learned world and by scholars who were friends and acquaintances of his. For the same reason most of the marital misery at the Steinhof in Lieme is also consigned to oblivion.

Despite the lack of such personal reactions, there are other indications of how highly even the little that was known of Kaempfer's work was appreciated. As early as 1704 Michael Bernhard Valentini, the well-known physician from Giessen, reprinted the chapters on dragon's

52. Frontispiece of the *Amoenitates exoticae*. The 'exotic tit-bits' from
Asia are presented to the allegorical figure of Europe, accompanied by
allegories of power (Neptune and Geography) – but also by Death.

blood resin and on Persian mummy from Kaempfer's dissertation in his
Museum Museorum.[19] No more could be expected before 1712, as Kaempfer had published nothing else.

During the last four years of his life the situation at the Steinhof appeared to become increasingly tense. Thus his first biographer wrote in the *Personalia oder Nachricht von dem Lebens-Lauffe des wohlsel. Herrn D. Kaempfers*: 'But at the beginning of this year [1716] he was again confined to bed following an extreme change, of which the less said the better, and, suffering more violently than ever before from colic, he had to allow himself in his continuing weakness to be brought here as an invalid at the end of January, in order to receive the necessary care.'[20] Although he recovered again to some extent that year, it seems that his vital energy must have been exhausted. Following severe pains and a prolonged indisposition he 'passed away quietly and blissfully in Jesus Christ on 2 November at 9 o'clock in the evening'.[21]

11. *The reception of Kaempfer in the eighteenth and nineteenth centuries*

During his own lifetime Kaempfer naturally did not exercise much influence, owing to the slow rate of his literary output. Nevertheless, he did live to see the publication of selective extracts from his dissertation in Valentini's work (above, p.92), but also the severe critique of his notes from Persepolis by De Bruijn (above, p.43). When Kaempfer died the greater part of his manuscripts and notes were still unedited. However, despite all the obstacles, he had succeeded in working up his Japanese notes into a publishable form. To be sure, it was only due to a stroke of great historical luck that this work was preserved, together with the rest of his literary remains.

The great English collector and naturalist Sir Hans Sloane (1660-1753)[1] possessed Kaempfer's dissertation and the *Amoenitates exoticae*. From the latter he knew that Kaempfer had brought a number of curiosities to Europe and that he was in possession of manuscript drafts for further works. When Sloane heard of Kaempfer's death he asked the personal physician to George I, Dr Johann Georg Steigerthal, to establish the whereabouts of his literary remains.[2] Steigerthal succeeded in coming to an arrangement with Kaempfer's sole heir, his nephew Dr Johann Hermann Kämpffer (1691-1736), and to purchase from him the oriental rarities as well as manuscripts and letters, in two lots (1723 and 1725), for

53. Sir Hans Sloane. (Portrait attributed to John Vanderbank.)

a total of 552 thaler. The manuscript of the work on Japan came to Sloane by way of the secretary of the Royal Society, Philip Henry Zollman (in reality, Philipp Heinrich Zollmann), who was paid 200 thaler (about £35 sterling) for it.[3]

To the learned Sloane the latter work, in particular, seemed so important that he urged Zollman to produce a translation. As the latter did not have the time for it, Sloane's Swiss amanuensis Johann Caspar Scheuchzer (1702-29) was given the task, which he rapidly completed. Thus Kaempfer's magnum opus could appear in London as early as 1727 in two volumes entitled *The History of Japan [...]*.[4] One may deplore the complex, decades-long history of publication that now ensued,[5] but the fact is that Scheuchzer's edition popularised Kaempfer's work in the scholarly and educated world of the eighteenth century: it went into a second English edition in 1728 and appeared in French in the Netherlands as early as 1729.[6] There were three further editions in the same language, as well as Dutch editions in 1729 and 1733.[7]

Not until 1753, however, did an extract appear in Schwabe's *Allgemeine Historie der Reisen zu Wasser und zu Lande [....]* and in 1756 another extract in the fourth section of Du Halde's *Ausführlicher Beschreibung des Chinesischen Reichs und der grossen Tartarey.*[8] Yet these texts had the disadvantage of not being based on Kaempfer's manuscript but on the French edition, which was itself derived from the English translation of Kaempfer's text.

This appeared to be a situation where nothing was likely to change, until Kaempfer's niece Maria Magdalena Kämpfer died in 1773. She had inherited her uncle's library from Johann Hermann.[9] When the books were checked – they had to be sold at auction as Maria Magdalena had died heavily in debt – two further manuscripts of the work on Japan were found, Johann Hermann having apparently withheld them from Dr Steigerthal. These were copies that had been made before the sale of the original documents to London.

In collaboration with the geographer Anton Friedrich Büsching (1734-93) and the publisher Christian Friedrich Helwing (1725-1800), proprietor of the prestigious Meyersche Hofbuchdruckerei in Lemgo (in which the *Amoenitates exoticae* had earlier been printed), the young Christian Wilhelm Dohm (1751-1820) published the first volume of his revised version of Kaempfer's manuscript in 1777 and the second volume in 1779.[10] It was in this form that Kaempfer's work on Japan was to be available in Germany right up to the present century.

The respect accorded to Kaempfer did not, of course, depend solely on Dohm's edition. Articles of some length were devoted to him in well-known biographical dictionaries such as those of Niceron (1732), Zedler (1737), Jöcher (1750) and Hirsching (1797). Even specialised reference works such as Kestner's *Medicinisches Gelehrten Lexicon [...]* or Iselin's *Neu vermehrtes historisch- und geographisches allgemeines Lexicon [...]* (1743) contain biographical sketches and a description of his works. Given the publishing history described above, however, it is understandable that the articles hardly ever provide any new information. The high regard in which Kaempfer was held within particular disciplines throughout Europe is also typical of the eighteenth century. As an example one could mention the English scholar Sir Joseph Banks (1743-1820), who in 1791 published a selection of Kaempfer's botanical drawings under the title *Icones selectae plantarum quas in Japonia collegit et delineavit Engelbertus Kaempferus.*[11] As his correspondence reveals, the volume was widely distributed, whether scientists requested copies or

54. Christian Wilhelm von Dohm (1751-1820), editor of the German translation of the *History of Japan*, published as *Geschichte und Beschreibung von Japan*.

Banks gave them away.[12] Moreover, for a long time Kaempfer's botanical descriptions and notices were a prime source and were used by, among others, such authorities as Linné and Thunberg.[13]

Kaempfer's work was also destined to have a widespread influence in the field of the history of ideas. Not only did Charlevoix, quite early on, include a detailed discussion of Kaempfer in his *Histoire et description générale du Japon* (Paris, 1736) (albeit with the aim of justifying the Catholic mission), but the information provided by Kaempfer ultimately formed the basis of the article on Japanese philosophy in the *Encyclopédie* of D'Alembert and Diderot.[14] His description of Japan was also influential in being used for the purpose of criticising European conditions.[15]

The 'homme illustre', as he was already described by Niceron, lost none of his significance even during the nineteenthth century. New writers naturally came to the fore and there were new endeavours to explore unknown regions and cultures more thoroughly. Yet all who dealt with fields where Kaempfer had already worked were obliged to come to terms with his painstaking labours. Thus Ritter not only characterises him as a 'master of the older period' of geographical description[16] but with regard, for example, to his account of southern Persia and above all of Bandar Abbas, which is important in terms of economic history, he concludes: 'We close with this information [primarily that of Kaempfer, but also of Mandelslo on Bandar Abbas], passing over the entire eighteenth century, which offers us no scientific increase in our geographical knowledge of that region [...].'[17]

It also, and above all, goes without saying that Kaempfer's influence did not wane in the fields of botany and pharmacology during the nineteenth century.[18] More importantly, however, his work on Japan was not forgotten, despite the researches of Siebold and Rein.[19] Moreover, it was not only in scientific publications that Kaempfer received the respect that he deserved, but through the reproduction of substantial passages from his description of Japan, with which subsequent authors embellished their works,[20] a wider reading public also continued to be aware of his enormous achievement.

12. *Karl Meier-Lemgo and Kaempfer studies in the twentieth century*

At the beginning of the twentieth century the reception of Kaempfer's work had slowed down somewhat, due to the fact that his papers still reposed as an unexplored treasure in the British Museum. It was Karl Meier (1882-1969)[1] who finally made the right move: in 1929 he travelled to London and examined the manuscripts there.[2] Only that study of the sources enabled him to produce the first detailed biography, *Engelbert Kaempfer, der erste Forschungsreisende, 1651 bis 1716: Leben, Reisen und Forschungen nach den bisher unveröffentlichten Handschriften Kaempfers im Britischen Museum bearbeitet*. Meier-Lemgo devoted his whole life to Kaempfer, describing his personality and achievement in numerous articles and books. It is not an exaggeration, therefore, to describe him as the doyen of modern Kaempfer studies. And it is undoubtedly due to him that Kaempfer now perhaps occupies a more prominent place in the history and literature of travel than he would have done in the absence of those publications.

In his efforts to produce a critical profile of Kaempfer he was limited by the fact that he attempted to define Kaempfer's personality only on the basis of his own subjective understanding and the viewpoint of the twentieth century.[3] It was certainly his abridged editions of the travel diaries and letters that first made these available to a wider scholarly audience,[4] but Meier-Lemgo treats Kaempfer's texts in a manner that is no longer tenable, in part reordering and regrouping them and acting on the belief that he had to improve their orthography and linguistic form. It is also true, of course, that it was only his dedicated work on the (in part almost illegible) notes that rescued that portion of Kaempfer's work from oblivion, yet by labelling him 'explorer', with all the consequences that flow from that in terms of the history of science, he has confined him to a role that he did not strictly speaking perform. As early as 1964, on the other hand, Beck chooses his words with care in his preface to the reprint of Dohm's edition of the work on Japan: 'His achievement consists in his having become the embodiment of the transition from discoverer to explorer at an important stage in the history of travel.'[5] It is possible for research to develop fruitfully only on the basis of such a discriminating approach.

The presentation below of further examples of the literature on Kaempfer is in no way meant to be regarded as aiming at exhaustive coverage but rather as a selective supplement to the material in Hüls' bibliography, highlighting works that have advanced or provided critical impulses for research in this field.

From the 1980s onward a new intensification of research can be identified. A high point, not only in scholarly but also in bibliographical terms, is the edition of the *Geschichte und Beschreibung von Japan* published by Springer-Verlag in 1980 together with Banks's *Icones* and a volume of commentary.[6] Dohm's text had indeed become known and accessible through Beck's 1964 edition, but it deserves to be emphasised that the reproduction of the Banksian selection of Kaempfer's botanical drawings brought the full range of his expertise to the notice of the scholarly world at a previously unknown qualitative level. The commentary part includes contributions by Scheuchzer, Kapitza, Hüls and Imai.[7] Apart from the essay by Scheuchzer, Kaempfer is presented in a new context in terms of the history of ideas (Kapitza, Hüls) while the need for a comprehensive analysis of the texts is argued at length for the first time by Imai.

The same year saw the publication of the extensive dissertation by the Viennese historian of cartography Margarete Lazar, *Engelbert Kaempfer als Kartograph und Geograph*, which for the first time presents a differentiated analysis of his maps and views. She again makes it clear that no statement of lasting validity can be made without recourse to the manuscripts – as Meier-Lemgo had already pointed out 51 years earlier.

Taking the outsider's viewpoint as his topic, Walther Hinz's pupil Berthold Spuler deals with Kaempfer's perspective on Persian culture. On Kaempfer's sojourn in Arabia there is an essay by Weisgerber.

In 1982 Hans Hüls and Hans Hoppe produced a large volume on the 330th anniversary of the traveller's birth which contains a number of interesting contributions.[8] An important feature is the translation of the *Valedictio* and the medical dissertation, though without the Latin text, and in the case of the latter without an explication of the bibliographical connection between the dissertation and the *Amoenitates exoticae*, this does not provide the basis for a deeper understanding. The identification – sadly never completed – of Kaempfer's route through Iran is of value for the history of geography; however, the addition of nearly 80 illustrations based on Kaempfer's drawings to supplement the text, due to Hüls' death, does make clear the extent to which these require interpretation by his texts. Hüls' analysis of Kaempfer's sojourn in Leiden is biographically informative. His bibliography brings together editions, translations and secondary literature to an unprecedented degree of completeness (672 titles).[9]

The reprint of the fifth section of the *Amoenitates* by Wolfgang Muntschick under the title of *Flora japonica* is indeed of value, but due to a number of extensive omissions it really calls for a revised edition.[10] In 1987 the same author published a translation of the fourth section of the *Amoenitates*, the history of the date palm, under the title of *Phoenix persicus*. The learned commentary demonstrates the significance of Kaempfer's studies not only for botany but for cultural history in general.[11]

Using the Siamese material as an example, Barend J. Terwiel creates a new image of Kaempfer as a scholarly writer who converted the basic material that he collected during his journeys into a 'consumable' form only after his return home; the changes that appear at that stage are not simply stylistic but of the greatest importance for understanding

Kaempfer's working method and his own aims and intentions.[12] Robert W. Carrubba discusses another specific problem in his essay 'Kaempfer's Latin account of the ordeal by fire in Siam' and also begins to fill another gap in that area by positioning this text of Kaempfer's among the travel accounts of the seventeenth century. He does the same, in collaboration with Bowers, with his study of Kaempfer's 'First report of the torpedo fish of the Persian Gulf'. No less important, though rarely studied, is the role of geology in Kaempfer's work. In this respect Kelbert breaks new ground with his essay on the Apsheron triad; such an essay demonstrates in an exemplary manner that what now attracts the attention only of specialists was of much wider interest to scholarly travellers three hundred years ago.

Of no less significance is the investigation of Kaempfer's milieu, his forerunners and contemporaries who devoted themselves to collecting plants in south-east and east Asia on behalf of the Dutch East India Company, a field in which Michel and Muntschick are making new contributions to our knowledge.[13]

Beatrice Bodart-Bailey has tackled problems connected with Kaempfer in several essays during the 1980s. In 'Warum noch einmal Kaempfer?' she examines the question of the place of the manuscript 'Heutiges Japan' (Sloane 3060) in the genesis of the work and evaluates the changes introduced by Dohm.[14] Elsewhere she deals with this question again in greater detail.[15] Whatever view one takes of the interrelationship between Kaempfer's various manuscripts, her pioneering work underlines the fact that only a critical edition of the surviving texts can clarify Kaempfer's aims and actual perceptions. In her essay 'Kyoto three hundred years ago' she subjects some topics of earlier research to renewed examination.

Among those with the most expert knowledge of Kaempfer's Japanese materials is Yu-Ying Brown. What Terwiel achieved with regard to the texts on Siam she has elaborated on the basis of the illustrations to 'Heutiges Japan' and their originals (in Sloane Add. Ms. 5252).[16] With great attention to detail she analyses the way in which Kaempfer reworked them. The detailed description and analysis of Kaempfer's printed and handwritten materials from Japan in her 1994 essay 'Japanese books and manuscripts' is a contribution towards an overall description of the Sloane collection. Such essays and investigations highlight the importance in this field, not only of source studies but of an understanding of the context of the collections of which the items form part.

Of more general interest are the short essay by Hanno Beck, 'Europa und Japan: zur Begegnung zweier Kulturen von 1295 bis zur Gegenwart', and 'Engelbert Kaempfers Reisen zu Wasser und zu Lande' by Hans Hoppe. Whereas Beck deals with the entire spectrum of European-Japanese contacts, following up previous studies,[17] Hoppe traces all Kaempfer's journeys without drawing any new conclusions, though his contribution provides a clear overview for a wider circle of readers.[18] Finally, the short article on Kaempfer in the *Kodansha Encyclopedia of Japan* by the doyen of historical research on voyages and the Dutch East India Company, Charles R. Boxer, also deserves mention.[19]

With the increasing differentiation of the literary canon, travel accounts are gradually coming within the purview of literary history. As a result, the interdisciplinary boundaries are shifting in favour of a productive discussion of genres and reception. In that sense Osterhammel's essay 'Reisen an die Grenzen der Alten Welt' is a typological contribution to defining the place of Kaempfer's work in the endeavours made during the seventeenth century to gain a perceptual mastery of the world. Osterhammel reveals motive forces to which far too little attention has hitherto been paid in the analysis of travel accounts. Brenner's survey *Der Reisebericht in der deutschen Literatur*, in which Kaempfer naturally occupies an important place, unfortunately appeared as early as 1990; he was therefore unable to take into account more recent literature on the subject. Brenner succeeds brilliantly, however, in summarising the research, listing desiderata and describing the relative significance of Kaempfer's writings (above all his work on Japan) in terms of comparative cultural and literary history.[20]

1990 was in many ways an important year for Kaempfer studies. On the 300th anniversary of his landing in Japan a major exhibition was mounted in four cities in Japan. The accompanying catalogue included some recently rediscovered documents from the Sloane collection in the British Library. Associated with this commemorative event, two notable international symposia were held in Lemgo and Tokyo, the proceedings of which were edited by the present writer as *Engelbert Kaempfer, Werk und Wirkung*. It would exceed the limits of this brief survey of research to deal individually with each of the twenty contributions.[21] Overall, it has made possible an entirely new general evaluation of the state of research. The lone scholar, such as Meier-Lemgo still was, endeavouring single-handedly to provide an all-round picture has been replaced by a multitude of scholars devoting themselves exclusively to particular disciplines.[22] From the investigation of the separate subject areas a panoptic view emerges that can hardly be surpassed in its variety. This brings out the multiple perspectives of the seventeenth century and the close association of the most varied fields of knowledge in the minds of individuals like Kaempfer.[23] The symposia of 1990 and their combined proceedings published in 1992 have also made another point abundantly clear: without a systematic, comprehensive and critical reappraisal of the sources – i.e. Kaempfer's printed works, his manuscripts, drawings and the objects he brought back from Asia – no valid statement can be made about his achievement.[24] Precisely because he was unable to bring his work to completion and left much of it in the form of sketches, drafts and half-completed texts it is imperative to provide a critical evaluation of these items of text and image, each of which lays claim to its own relative significance as a fragment of an unrealised whole, and to draw conclusions from the evolution of the text as to Kaempfer's perceptions and mode of presentation. Only in that way can the '*curiositas*' to which Kaempfer devotes himself be demonstrated and evaluated in detail.[25]

Interdisciplinary research reveals Kaempfer overall as a leading source for the history of seventeenth-century science, travel and culture. The present biography of Kaempfer, in which the writer subjected the sources and research findings to a new examination more than fifty years after that of Meier-Lemgo,[26] likewise appeared in 1990. One of its most significant conclusions is that the myth of Kaempfer as an 'exploring' traveller, who all along had Japan as his goal, is untenable. It only became so in the course of his travels around the Dutch East India Company's empire and ultimately resulted from the succession of professional setbacks that he experienced. The inferences to be drawn from that with regard to an evaluation of his studies, some of which are already emerging from the critical work on the manuscripts, cannot yet be predicted in detail.

The present writer's contribution in the same year to *Kulturvermittler zwischen Japan und Deutschland* establishes the important place occupied by Kaempfer in the ranks of those who advanced our knowledge of Japan. Through the numerous textual extracts and cross-references in the anthology *Japan in Europa* Peter Kapitza above all traces the ramifications of Kaempfer's influence, which is by no means limited to the reception of the *History of Japan*.[27]

Finally, with regard to the research undertaken since 1990, a few more works need to be discussed. Wolfgang Caesar's specialised study on the ginseng root, 'Ginsengwurzel in Europa', is of interest, as he defined

Kaempfer's place in the history of the investigation of that medicinal plant. Supplementing his contribution in the proceedings of the 1990 symposia, Wiesehöfer outlines Kaempfer's understanding of the Achaemenid sites in Persia. Landwehr offers a minute bibliographical analysis of the *Amoenitates*, the work on Japan and other texts in the context of publications relating to the Company.[28] He has for the first time made possible an exact overview of the foliation and illustration of the works in question.

In 1992 the volume of conference proceedings edited by Josef Kreiner, *Kenperu no mita Tokugawa-Japan*, was published by the Rokko Shuppan company, containing nineteen contributions and with a different focus from the proceedings of the 1990 symposia.[29] This volume shows again that there still remains a whole series of instructive topics that have not yet been investigated. For Japan and Japanese scholars this commendable volume contains a number of informative reports that would probably not otherwise have been brought together.

For the history of moxibustion and acupuncture before and during the lifetime of Kaempfer essential clarifications appear to have been achieved. Here it is above all Wolfgang Michel who has most recently examined this area of mutual Japanese-European interaction in a series of essays.[30] In this connection reference should be made to his earlier essay 'Engelbert Kaempfer's merkwürdiger Moxa-Spiegel', in which he vividly describes the barriers to the reception of a medical practice that was completely unintelligible to Europeans.

Also deserving notice is Margot Massey's essay on Kaempfer as a chronicler of the Edo period, which essentially provides an overview of his life, travels and research, supplemented with some notes on the *suzuri* producers and the *fugu* fish. In view of the copious and complex international literature on this topic to date Massey, in certain respects, falls short of expectations.[31] However, the structure of her essay confirms the significance of the many relationships and connections that are still worth examining: scholarly activities spanning Europe and Asia, commerce and the republic of letters.[32] Such connections are also described by the present writer for a wider audience in a series of articles that provide introductory information with suggestions for further reading.[33]

On the 450th anniversary of the beginning of European-Japanese relations the Berlin Festival of 1993 presented the ambitious exhibition *Japan und Europa 1543-1929*, with a catalogue of the same title. A contribution by the present writer examines the question of Kaempfer's working method. The analysis shows that it falls somewhere between a receptivity directed mainly towards the remarkable and bizarre, and scholarly observation of an alien culture. It is the encyclopaedic scope of his quest that is significant, not his errors or what he failed to observe due to the circumstances in which he found himself.[34]

In 1994 Carruba dealt in an unexpected place with a topic of only seeming marginality: 'Pastor H. G. Weland's Latin elegy for Engelbert Kaempfer'. The analysis of the epicedium, supplementing that of Haccius' funeral sermon,[35] reveals the unmediated contemporary perception of Kaempfer's life – a matter of crucial importance in view of the many subsequent interpretations of his work and life.

Terwiel draws attention in the *IIAS Newsletter* to the British Library as the location of Kaempfer's Siamese manuscripts.[36] In the same issue the present writer also describes the significance of Kaempfer's writings and the need for international collaboration to exploit these buried treasures in the British Library.[37]

The same year saw the appearance of a short monograph by Bodart-Bailey, the title of which – *Kaempfer and Tokugawa Tsunayoshi: die Kontakte eines deutschen Arztes mit dem Shôgun* – suggests merely an account of a particular episode in his life whereas in fact it offers more, namely a full biography; his Japanese experiences occupy about a third of the book. This work would certainly fill a gap for Japanese readers.[38]

A volume of essays entitled *The furthest goal: Engelbert Kaempfer's encounter with Tokugawa Japan*, edited by Beatrice Bodart-Bailey and Derek Massarella, was published in January 1996, providing welcome evidence of the continuing interest in Kaempfer's work.[39] It includes contributions by the editors as well as by Wolfgang Muntschick, Jörg Schmeisser and Paul van der Velde, though these have already appeared elsewhere. The essay by Carmen Blacker[40] and the postscript by Derek Massarella[41] are new and illuminating. The biographical sketch by Bodart-Bailey does not add anything new, whereas her essay on the genesis of the *History of Japan*[42] reveals significant details about the relationship between scholars and merchants in Asia. It is to be regretted that more academics were not persuaded to contribute to the volume, which might then have presented a really comprehensive rather than somewhat uneven study of Japan in the Tokugawa period.

13. *The way ahead*

The multitude of works and projects inevitably raises the question of a synthesis. One answer might be that the many fragments available to us in the form of Kaempfer's published work and notes should be used to create a whole, not in the sense of the 'complete structure' that Meier-Lemgo still believed he could produce[1] but in the sense of a presentation of all the texts and materials for the purpose of further, text-based research.

The best way of making available such a collection of the most diverse texts (from the incidental marginal note to the printed book) is of course by means of a complete edition. The preparation of such an edition has begun under the title of *Engelbert Kaempfer, Werke: kritische Ausgabe der gedruckten und ungedruckten Schriften*. The varied and fragmentary nature of the manuscripts left behind by Kaempfer, which are several times greater in quantity than the printed portion of his output, made it necessary to adopt a mixed editorial policy. The texts are published on the basis of tested methods of literary editing, guided by the 'principle of the latest hand'.[2] This is based on the unambiguous conclusion that Kaempfer wished to present the public of his day with a self-contained, fully formulated and definitive text, as he did on the basis of his research in the case of the *Amoenitates*. The preservation of some drafts of the latter in Sloane 2907 clearly indicates that he gave priority to the printed text while the drafts were of less importance; their preservation is thus fortuitous and fragmentary.

Although individual texts are conventionally presented, with a main text, critical apparatus and selective commentary, the material as a whole demands a departure from the traditional chronological or genre-based arrangement. The edition therefore begins with the completed *Amoenitates* of 1712. In that work the author's aim is expressed with particular clarity, as Kaempfer revised and expanded his dissertation of 1694 in order to present it to the educated public in this context as an 'oriental gem'. Moreover, in the preface he refers to his forthcoming works.

Whereas the *Amoenitates* were already printed during the author's lifetime, that was not the case with 'Heutiges Japan. Zu einer Zweifachen

Hoff-Reise durchgeschauet und beschrieben etc.' (Sloane 3060), the manuscript that formed the basis for Scheuchzer's revision of the text as the *History of Japan*. At the time of Kaempfer's death it was not yet quite ready for printing but would most likely have been the next to be published. The situation is very different with regard to the travel notes and the linguistic, botanical and geographical notes. These represent raw materials which can indeed be placed in rough chronological order but cannot always be unequivocally related to already completed parts of his work. In the case of the letters (Sloane 3063, 3064) even material that Kaempfer would scarcely have published has been preserved. For that reason it makes more sense in this case to provide access to the material by subject areas and within these, if necessary, by regions.[3] Here only the critical editing[4] and commentary will show the relative significance to which the individual text can lay claim within the history of each particular discipline.[5]

In that sense the 'Humboldt of the seventeenth century'[6] still remains to a large extent a *terra incognita*. His writings represent one of the important achievements in the history of travel and science as he succeeded, without systematic preparation, in gaining access conceptually to not one but several, quite distinct cultures. This is attributable not so much to some vague genius but to his intelligence, which was sturdy and inclined towards the concrete. In addition to his creative and organising abilities he had a talent for describing things by drawing and writing. Thanks to the latter, combined with his extensive knowledge and linguistic skills, he has exercised an influence beyond his own time. That, too, derives from his effort not merely to describe natural phenomena but also to grasp each culture in its current and historical context. In this respect, as well, the relative significance of his work should not be underestimated.

Also of importance, therefore, is his working method, which is consistently based on a scholarly impulse and stands on the threshold of modern scientific practice, as Kaempfer combined accuracy, circumspection and far-sightedness with resourcefulness and determination. Due to the difficult circumstances of his life, however, he was denied the kind of success enjoyed by the incomparably more fortunate Alexander von Humboldt. Even his posthumous fame cannot disguise the fact that he failed to complete his work owing to the unsettled conditions of the time and perhaps also his own fastidiousness.

The words of the Enlightenment scholar Albrecht von Haller still carry the expression of praise that has always applied to exceptional and outstanding personalities: '*Nulli peregrinatorum secundus ad omnem laborem impiger neque sibi parcens quoties veri detegendi spes erat.*' Second to none among travellers, he was undeterred by any toil, nor did he spare himself when there was a chance of discovering the truth.

Notes

2 Family, youth and schooldays

1 On the family history, see Meier-Lemgo, *Geschichte*, pp.192-203. A detailed account is given by Flaskamp, *Persien*, pp.85-7.

2 The historian Franz Flaskamp, in particular, has retained this form of the name, with a certain rigidity. See Flaskamp, *Persien*, p.87f. and *Quellen*, p.171f.

3 Quoted from Flaskamp, *Quellen*, p.171, n.6.

4 Kaempfer's correspondents write the name in a great variety of ways. Raphael du Mans writes 'Kemper' and 'Kempher'; Lycochthon uses 'Kempfer', the form under which he also appears in the muster roll of the 'Pampus', on which he returned to Europe in 1693; finally, the form 'Cempher' also occurs. (All in: Sloane 3064.)

5 Nordrhein-westfälisches Staatsarchiv Detmold, L 16 O K.

6 Kaempfer's nephew entered his name as a matter of course as 'Johann Hermann Kämpfer, Lemgoviensis' in the register of the grammar school. Quoted from Flaskamp, *Quellen*, p.172, n.10.

7 *Exercitatio*, p.27. In the supplement to the funeral sermon for Joachim his name is interpreted in the same sense: 'The fight is over now/oh thou! dear Kaempffer brave!' *Leich-Predigt Joachim Kaempffer*, p.74. [The German word *Kämpfer* means 'fighter' or 'warrior' (Transl.)]

8 Haccius, p.14. In the full title of the funeral sermon the religious approach becomes particularly clear when he describes Kaempfer's life and death as 'the best journey of a Christian warrior towards the celestial East'.

9 On the general situation, see Kittel, p.109. 'The town of Lemgo, where the number of houses in 1618 had been 1057, possessed only 590 by 1648; of their 4665 inhabitants in the year 1629 only 1372 remained. The loss in terms of levies, ransoms and plunder was estimated for Lemgo alone at 1382 million Thaler.' On the situation throughout the empire, see also Braubach, pp.13-25.

10 Their success proved him right: Joachim became an official receiver in Goslar, Johann a Bavarian councillor and high bailiff and Andreas a vicar and Hebrew scholar. Hoppe probably describes Johannes Kemper's educational aims accurately when he writes: 'In its educational ambitions the Kemper family identified with absolutism, and the father already cultivated his connections with the counts of Lippe. [...] In the second half of the seventeenth century the scholarly virtues were no longer sufficient in themselves for a successful career, which now also demanded the qualities of a man of the world with courtly manners.' Hoppe, *Gesellschaft*, p.136.

11 On the library, see Flaskamp, *Bücherkauf*, pp.126-222. With its 1137 items, it represents more than just the father's library, as Joachim's and Engelbert's acquisitions were included.

12 Hoppe, *Gesellschaft*, p.137. On the general aims of the schools in the seventeenth century, see Paulsen, vol.1, pp.492-505.

13 Haccius, p.46.

14 Hoppe, *Gesellschaft*, p.139f.

15 Meier-Lemgo, *Biographie*, p.15. In his suggestive formulations he goes to almost any lengths to create a psychological profile, despite the absence of any unequivocal evidence from Kaempfer himself on which to base it.

16 Hoppe, *Gesellschaft*, p.137.

17 On this matter, see also the detailed account by Kleinwegener, p.21f. On Kemper's official duties in a recorded case, ibid., p.43.

18 Precisely because this was customary, it is hardly likely that Kaempfer had a special inclination towards the 'profession' of a 'scientific' traveller – quite apart from the fact that foreign journeys were undertaken only when absolutely necessary. See Hoppe's listing of the pupils in Lemgo who came from elsewhere, p.138. Besides, evidence for this particular choice of profession among young persons in the seventeenth century is likely to be extremely hard to find.

19 On Johannes Kemper's position, see Hoppe, *Gesellschaft*, p.134. Meier-Lemgo, *Geschichte*, p.111f. On his retirement from office, Meier-Lemgo, *Geschichte*, p.112, compared with Flaskamp, *Quellen*, p.87 and Hoppe, *Gesellschaft*, p.135f.

20 Whatever significance one attaches to the passage quoted above from the funeral sermon as one of the earliest sources for Kaempfer's life, one should not forget that, apart from (possibly) reflecting such an inclination, it was also influenced by Kaempfer's life, by then already concluded, the culmination of which – the long sojourn abroad – was a subject of general interest, not to say unmerciful curiosity, during his final years. Moreover, as regards their content, funeral sermons followed prescribed forms and rhetorical rules which had to be observed. On this, see Fürstenwald, p.458f. See also Winkler's elucidation of the allegorical purpose and extravagant praise in funeral sermons: Winkler, pp.127, 134f., 156ff., as well as p.238. (This throws an interesting light on Haccius's funeral sermon as a biographical source.) On the tradition and form of the epicedium (elegy) and parentation (memorial oration) in relation to the funeral sermon, see Lenz, pp.143-61.

21 Haccius, p.53. This passage accords with the tradition that he involved himself in pastoral concerns. On this, see Butterweck, p.489.

22 See Hoppe, *Gesellschaft*, p.135f. In this connection no account can be taken of his attitude to the witchcraft trials, as there is no sure evidence for his own view, which was surely one of disapproval, as we know only from Puhstkuchen's (sic!) *Beyträgen* (a late but reliable source).

3 The years of study

1 See Ostermeyer. Like the Flörcke family, the Protts were one of the families that had moved from Lemgo to Hameln and had produced councillors and mayors there since the sixteenth century. Joachim married a Maria Magdalena Prott in 1690. Jöcher wrongly gives the place as Hanau: Jöcher, pt.2, col.2043. According to another early biography : 'cumque puer etiam mirum peregre abeundi alien-

asque oras visendi proderet studium, Hanoviam [!] primo.' Krause, p.64.

2 Haccius does not mention this journey. With Dohm the notion that Kaempfer had been born to travel was already so entrenched that he writes: 'The urge to travel, which accompanied him throughout his life, now induced the seventeen-year-old Kaempfer to make a short journey to Holland.' *Geschichte und Beschreibung von Japan*, vol.I, p.xvf. He can provide no further particulars about this journey either. A possible date would be when he transferred from the grammar school in Hameln to the one in Lüneburg. Dohm's perception of his 'urge to travel' can be explained in terms of the status accorded to travel during the Enlightenment; one has only to think of Nicolai's journey in Germany and Switzerland. His brother Joachim's periods of study in Leiden and Utrecht were at a later date. See *Leich-Predigt Joachim Kaempffer*, Personalia, pp.39-42.

3 Meier-Lemgo's explanation for his later decision to go to Sweden sounds rather unconvincing in connection with this journey: 'Which country's service should he enter? Holland at that time was swarming with scholars. So Kaempfer sought his fortune in Sweden.' Meier-Lemgo, *Mann des Willens*, p.328. It is hard to believe that, after years of study at school and university, Kaempfer would have let himself be guided by such a distant experience in his youth.

4 Haccius, p.47. On Kettenbeil see Jöcher, suppl. vol. 3, col.285f. On the importance of the education system in Lüneburg and its wider influence after the Thirty Years' War, see Reinecke, vol.II, pp.287-94.

5 'became fairly *profectus ... tam in musica vocali quam instrumentali*'. Haccius, p.47.

6 Kaempfer was wise to cultivate this talent, which was not merely a part of social life, as the genre paintings of the period show us, but of the skills of a private tutor – and it was in the latter capacity that he would later have to earn his living. The novelist and musician Johann Beer vividly described this feature of contemporary life: 'For resounding music is far more conducive to pleasure than delicate ticklings of the ear, which offer neither meat nor drink.' Beer, p.139.

7 *Phoenix persicus*, pp.154ff.

8 *Geschichte und Beschreibung von Japan*, vol.I, p.xvi.

9 On the significance of the Lübeck grammar school in north Germany, see Paulsen, vol.I, p.323.

10 Jöcher, vol.3, col.986; suppl. vol. 5, col.836f.

11 Paulsen, vol.I, p.323.

12 On Keckermann see Beck, *Geographie*, p.115. On Keckermann's influence see Kastrop, pp.79-87.

13 See Jöcher, vol.3, col.876.

14 See the introduction to the *Exercitatio*, p.15.

15 The best-known among the names referred to by Kaempfer are Keckermann, Hermann Conring, Wilhelm Witzendorff and Johannes Linnaeus.

16 *Exercitatio*, p.25f.

17 *Exercitatio*, p.26f.

18 Meier-Lemgo, *Leben*, p.264f.

19 See Werner Conze's article 'Monarchie' in: *Geschichtliche Grundbegriffe: historisches Lexicon zur politisch-sozialen Sprache in Deutschland*, eds. Otto Brunner,

Werner Conze, Reinhart Koselleck, vol.4, Stuttgart, 1978, pp.168-89; especially pp.173-84.

20 See Hoppe, *Gesellschaft*, p.136, on the attitude of Kaempfer's father towards absolutism.

21 Contrary to what Meier-Lemgo says, Kaempfer does not cite the famous theoretician of natural law Hugo Grotius. Meier-Lemgo, *Leben*, p.264. One can hardly make Kaempfer out to be a philosopher on the basis of this little work and the chapter on Japan's justification for its exclusion policy towards other countries.

22 See the *Stammbuch*, pp.147-54. In this he was following a widespread custom that had been practised since the fifteenth century.

23 Even in Dohm's biographical sketch the distance in time is perceptible – some eighty years having elapsed since Kaempfer's death – as he already depended on second-hand sources and judged Kaempfer from the standpoint of the enlightened bourgeoisie. His account is nevertheless important, as he clearly still had access to documents which must now be regarded as lost. See *Geschichte und Beschreibung von Japan*, vol.I, p.xv, note. Scheuzer's Life of Kaempfer is included in his edition of Kaempfer's *History of Japan*.

24 *Geschichte und Beschreibung von Japan*, vol.I, p.xvi. Meier-Lemgo's statement that 'In Torun he continued his education in 1674' thus covers the facts only very loosely. *Stammbuch*, p.146. Kaempfer's decision to stay in Torun for a considerable time was not merely due to the fact that the city 'lay on the route' between Danzig and Cracow. For Torun was not only the birthplace of Copernicus but, after the troubles of the sixteenth century, it possessed a first-rate grammar school whose influence extended far beyond its borders. Lutheranism had also been permitted here by royal decree, so that Torun had the undisputed reputation of being an 'evangelical' city. Heuer, p.10f. Klimaszewski, p.119: 'Amongst them [i.e. higher level secondary schools] the academic gymnasium at Torun, where lectures were held by graduates of the universities of Leipzig, Basel and Leiden, got ahead of other Protestant gymnasiums at Gdansk and Elblag.'

25 *Stammbuch*, p.147.

26 ibid.

27 ibid.

28 On the development of Cracow university until the sixteenth and seventeenth centuries, see Hartmann, pp.42ff. Klimaszewski, p.118f., only emphasises the high standard of mathematics. On the history of universities in general see Estreicher. It is surely unjustified to describe the level of medical science as entirely 'scholastic', meaning that it was not open to new ideas. In assessing the state of affairs, one should remember that knowledge of the subject and methods changed slowly everywhere in the seventeenth century. See Diepgen, vol.1, p.317.

29 See especially entry no. 6a and nos. 7, 8, 10 and 11. *Stammbuch*, pp.148-51. The length of his sojourn is wrongly stated in Haccius, p.47.

30 Haccius, p.47. Compare Krause's statement with reference to Cracow, 'ubi per triennium viam [...] egregie institit, & insignes in Philosophicis pariter atque in cognitione linguarum exoticarum, populorum, regionumque fecit progressus.' Krause, p.64.

31 Haccius merely says: 'and there [...] he also achieved *supremum in philosophia gradum* with credit.' Haccius, p.47. See Krause, p.64; Zedler, col.40; Jöcher, vol.2, col.2043. Dohm gives no source for his assertion that Kaempfer obtained the title of master of arts. *Geschichte und Beschreibung von Japan*, vol.I, p.xvi. See also Flaskamp, *Persien*, p.89.

With regard to the Cracow archives, Tell has established that, due to wartime destruction, no elucidation can be expected from there. His enquiry, it is true, relates to Kaempfer's friendship with Baron Klingenstierna, but the same conclusion is likely to apply to other university records. See Tell, *Stormaktsdiplomat*, p.4.

32 The dates relate to the entries in the album amicorum. See *Stammbuch*, pp.152ff.

33 *Geschichte und Beschreibung von Japan*, vol.I, p.xvi.

34 The entry in the university register reads 'Kämpffer, Engelbert[us], Lemchaven[sis] Westphal[us], iur.' Erler, p.101.

35 *Stammbuch*, pp.160-2. Similarly Dohm: 'In Königsberg, however, Kaempfer devoted himself principally to pharmaceutics.' *Geschichte und Beschreibung von Japan*, vol.I, p.xvi.

36 Flaskamp, *Persien*, p.90, who attempts to find evidence for this opinion in the album amicorum (ibid., p.160ff.). The entries concerned (nos.33-9), however, are only those of theologians and medical men.

37 'From Cracow, with his father's approval, he went to the Prussian university at Königsberg where he pursued the *studium medicum* for four whole years with all diligence and great application.' Haccius, p.47f. Dohm writes: 'Here [in Königsberg] he remained for four years, during which he acquired, in particular, the rather unusual knowledge of a subject which at that time was still relatively unknown – namely natural history, which subsequently became so important to him during his travels, and for the enrichment of which he brought back such interesting materials.' *Geschichte und Beschreibung von Japan*, vol.I, p.xvi.

38 On the history of Königsberg in the second half of the seventeenth century, see Franz, pp.137-43; Gause, vol.I, pp.454-552.

39 Franz (see above, note 38), p.148.

40 Its main representatives were Simon Dach (1605-59), Robert Robertin (1616-48), Christoph Caldenbach (1613-98), Rutger zum Bergen (1603-61) and Johann Peter Titz (1619-89). They, as well as others not listed here, belonged to the most diverse professions, so that for that reason alone there could well have been a lively exchange of ideas. See Gause (above, note 38), pp.465-71. Titz wrote an entry in Kaempfer's album in June 1676, which throws a significant light on his active involvement in the cultural life of Danzig. See *Stammbuch*, p.153f.

41 On the development of Sweden into a Baltic power as a result of the religious changes and the rule of Sigismund III (1587-1632), see Manthey, pp.116-20. On Lemgo's relations with Sweden, see Gaul, pp.197-200.

42 'I had scarcely been there two years when I had to return home, and my studies were utterly interrupted. My second brother [Engelbert] came from Königsberg in Prussia, and he persuaded my father that I should accompany him to Königsberg, where I would be able to manage. When we arrived in Lübeck we were told that our funds were insufficient, we had to part and one of us travel to Stockholm.

I realised that my brother could not get away, so I boarded a ship and travelled to Stockholm and let my brother go to Prussia.' See Andreas Kempffer's autobiography, in Baur, p.15.

43 See Hüls, *Promotion*, p.186. One must also to take into account the one and three quarter years during which he may not have been studying.

44 See the letter written after his return home in 1694, Sloane 3063, 41r, and *Geschichte und Beschreibung von Japan*, vol.I, p.lxiiif. The situation after August 1682, following his father's death, is described in the laconic words of Andreas: 'but this was my misfortune, that the money I earned in Sweden was soon spent. Opportunities are scarce. In the meantime my father had died. No money came from Westphalia.' Andreas Kempffer's autobiography, in Baur, p.16.

45 *Geschichte und Beschreibung von Japan*, vol.I, p.xvi. Even the famous Simon Dach – and many others – made a living (not unsuccessfully!) by giving private tuition.

46 In Königsberg one Johann Ritter wrote an entry in his album as late as August. See *Stammbuch*, p.155f. Whether Kaempfer necessarily travelled to Lübeck by sea, as Meier-Lemgo firmly assumes (*Stammbuch*, p.155), is doubtful, as the journey by land was cheaper.

47 *Stammbuch*, p.156.

48 *Stammbuch*, p.157f.

49 'Then Kaempfer's love of travel took him to Sweden': thus Massey believed, even in 1968, that his move to Scandinavia could be explained (Massey, *Kaempfer alive!* p.103). Similarly Hoppe, with a rather convoluted argument: 'His early acquaintance with Holland must have taught him that the Baltic was an important centre of global trade relations with the East.' Hoppe, *Gesellschaft*, p.139.

4 From Sweden to Persia

1 On his scientific achievements, see Zedler, vol.32, col.1448-50. As was the case with a number of baroque scholars, his talent for exact research was mingled with an inclination towards the obscure (he wanted to prove, for example, that all nations were descended from the Swedes). See also the article by S. Lindroth on Rudbeck in *Svenska män och kvinnor*, vol.6, pp.382-5.

2 Despite Dohm's surmise 'that, had it not been for Rudbeck, he [Kaempfer] might never have thought of tracing the route of the first Japanese from the tower of Babel to the eastern coast of Asia' (*Geschichte und Beschreibung von Japan*, vol.I, p.xviif.), such an influence can hardly be proved in this particular instance.

3 Holsten, p.20.

4 The question as to how scientific currents and methods may have affected his work must be left open at this point and can be answered only by an examination of the original texts. It is interesting, however, that there was a copy of Descartes' *Discours de la méthode* (Leiden, 1637) in Kaempfer's library. See *Catalogus*, p.29, no.72. Simplifying the matter, one might say that Descartes' method of exact observation and rational deduction can be recognised in the nature of Kaempfer's observations. Rather than indulging in vague conjectures, Kaempfer first describes and classifies the observable phenomena before drawing conclusions.

5 Rudbeck, the brothers Pufendorf and the university librarian, Olaus Verelius, all wrote entries in the album. See *Stammbuch*, p.163f.
6 *Geschichte und Beschreibung von Japan*, vol.I, p.xviii. This is expressed more concisely, though no less aptly, in his funeral oration: 'In the same way he apparently devoted himself to the *studiis academicis* at Uppsala in Sweden in such a laudable manner that it also brought him into special consideration at the Swedish court.' Haccius, p.48.
7 *Geschichte und Beschreibung von Japan*, vol.I, p.xviii. Here Dohm obviously relies on lost sources, for no proof of such a promise could be found even by enquiries in Sweden. Tell's investigations in Sweden were apparently also fruitless. See Tell, *Tysk läkare*, p.125.
8 See Olearius, ed. by Dieter Lohmeier, pp.10*-12*. Precisely this had already been the aim of the notable legation from Holstein that had spent the years 1633-9 on its journey. It had not actually achieved its commercial objectives but, quite apart from its original purpose, the account given of it by Olearius had brought it wide renown.
9 *Reisetagebücher*, p.5. See Hoppe, *Missionen*. Fabritius did propose a treaty to the Persians in 1679 but it had not resulted in any trade. See also the authoritative work by Troebst, p.165f.
10 This is evident from the Swedish offer to Sulayman. See Sloane 3063, 123v f. On the Swedish legation in relation to the activities of other states, see Sibylla Schuster-Walser, pp.59-80, esp. p.79f.
11 The dates given below are taken from Kaempfer's travel diary and no further separate references will be given. Meier-Lemgo's edition is still the only available version of Kaempfer's diaries and thus indispensable. See *Reisetagebücher*, p.2.
12 On the route through Finland, see Lunelund.
13 *Reisetagebücher*, p.12.
14 ibid. See also Fabritius's letter to his employers of 22.6.1683. Sloane 3063, 97r f.
15 *Reisetagebücher*, p.20f.
16 ibid., p.22. On the significance of Kaempfer's description of the Tsars and Russian conditions in general, see Loewensohn, pp.663-6.
17 *Reisetagebücher*, p.24.
18 *Reisetagebücher*, p.26f.
19 See *Stammbuch*, pp.168ff.; *Reisetagebücher*, p.27f.
20 Sloane 3063, 112v f. ('Der Kürbis einverleibet'.)
21 Not only is Meier-Lemgo's reading 'einer Kürbis einverleibet' [carved on a gourd-bottle] meaningless and wrong, but his conclusion that Kaempfer worked 'entirely within the conventions of the mannered versifying of his time' is also one-sided and inappropriate. See Meier-Lemgo, *Biographie*, p.23. In the same way as with Kaempfer one finds travel motifs and emblematics in the poems of Paul Fleming, who accompanied Olearius on his journey to Persia. On Fleming's poems see Olearius, ed. by Detlef Haberland, pp.41ff.
22 *Emblemata*, col.181. On the gourd as a symbol for the transitory, see also Schöne, pp.16ff.
23 The text of the travel diary does not make it entirely clear when the Swedish

legation hired a vessel. The passage in which Kaempfer describes this may possibly be the particular one that is illegible. See *Reisetagebücher*, p.29. That they did use a boat is shown only by the expression 'Passed by the village of Resan' [Ryazan?]. ibid.

24 *Reisetagebücher*, p.31.

25 *Geschichte und Beschreibung von Japan*, vol.I, p.xxvif.

26 See Olearius, ed. by Dieter Lohmeier, p.45 * f. See also the introduction by Meier-Lemgo to his Kaempfer edition: 'Presented here (in chronological order) are first the original notes made during the journey, followed by later entries written as fair copy. The existing text has been preserved as far as possible but, in view of the immensely complex paragraphs and the constant mingling of German and Latin, some effort had to be made to turn it into readable German. I think I can say, however, that I have faithfully reproduced the sense of Kaempfer's text throughout.' *Reisetagebücher*, p.2. This passage reveals the problem with Meier-Lemgo's edition, which can be quoted only with reservations. Meier-Lemgo not only fails to identify the 'original notes' and the 'entries written as fair copy', he also freely combines various texts, linking the travel diaries with the *Amoenitates exoticae* by conjecturing 'which sections it is most plausible – for it is impossible to be completely certain here – that Kaempfer might have included in his *Itinerarium*'. (*Reisetagebücher*, ibid.) Such an approach is quite inadmissible on philological grounds and in this case even misleading. It is, after all, known from the preface to his *Amoenitates* that Kaempfer, apart from his other works, planned a 'Hodoeporicum tripartitum in folio', the scope of which he did not envisage as being in any way restricted by the already completed *Amoenitates*. See *Amoenitates exoticae*, p.[xiii]. In what manner Kaempfer might conceivably have included parts of the *Amoenitates* in this travel account can only be conjectured. Only a critical edition of the travel diaries would enable one to be more specific about Kaempfer's intentions and procedures.

27 *Stammbuch*, p.172.

28 See for example Haccius, p.49, Jöcher, vol.2, col.2043; no longer in suppl. vol.3 of the latter, pp.9ff.

29 *Reisetagebücher*, p.38.

30 On the seventeenth-century route through Persia see Gabriel, p.109f.

31 Olearius, ed. by Dieter Lohmeier, p.418f.

32 *Reisetagebücher*, pp.51ff. *Amoenitates exoticae*, pp.262ff.

33 On this matter generally, see the excellent though unfortunately incomplete reconstruction of Kaempfer's route through Persia by Hüls. Hüls, *Spuren*, p.167.

34 On the caravan routes see Gabriel, p.110, as well as the detailed maps in Hüls, *Spuren*, p.168.

35 For instance, in describing the town of Qum he writes: 'Olearius drew a plan of the town which, however, resembles it as much as a cow does a windmill.' *Reisetagebücher*, p.76. Among the travel books in his father's library that were printed before Engelbert's departure from Lemgo the work by Pietro della Valle (*Beschryving der Reizen*, Amsterdam, 1666) is especially noteworthy. (*Catalogus*, p.28, no.48.) He may possibly have read various other works in some of the libraries of the schools and universities that he attended.

36 *Reisetagebücher*, p.77.
37 See likewise Helga Schutte Watt, p.51f.
38 *Reisetagebücher*, p.42.
39 ibid., p.82.
40 ibid., p.84.
41 ibid., p.78.
42 ibid., p.61f.
43 ibid., p.66.
44 On the history of geographical theory see Beck, *Geschichte*, pp.6-10. Beck, *Geographie*, the introductions to the individual source texts.
45 Meier-Lemgo repeatedly deplores the 'constant mixing of German and Latin' (*Reisetagebücher*, p.2) or Kaempfer's faulty education in German (*Biographie*, p.162). It is not fair to say that he preferred Latin because he found it 'easier to express himself in that than in his own mother tongue'. (*Briefe*, p.9.) On the contrary, the alternation between the languages was an intellectual decision and was used intentionally.
46 On this see Spuler.
47 *Amoenitates exoticae*, ed. by Walther Hinz, p.15f.
48 'The only reliable source remains the summary account by Kaempfer from the end of the seventeenth century. It can be accepted unhesitatingly, as Kaempfer has proved to be extremely reliable in his reporting and has recorded his observations with a precision that even today fulfils the requirements of scientific accuracy.' Würfel, p.35.
49 *Amoenitates exoticae*, ed. by Walther Hinz, p.156f.
50 ibid., p.159f.
51 ibid., p.167f.
52 On this see Homayoun, who deals with Kaempfer's drawings and engravings in relation to other representations of Persian subjects. Throughout he notes the quality of Kaempfer's drawings and their superiority over those of other travellers.
53 His real name was Jacques Dutertre, from Le Mans. Flaskamp, *Persien*, p.92. See also *Lexicon Capucinum*, col.1445.
54 Under Sulayman, however, he no longer dared to appear at court as the latter, in contrast to his father Abbas II, did not show such a liberal attitude towards the monk. The missionary zeal of du Mans, as well as his openly revealed contempt for Islam, also appears to have increased with the passage of time. His report 'Estat de la Perse en 1660', which he compiled for Colbert, is well informed but has a 'strongly missionary' bias. See Schuster-Walser, pp.19f., 36, 57, 66, 91, 115.
55 Turkish was the language of the court and the administration. See Sloane 2908.
56 ibid.
57 On this, see Troebst, pp.166-70. Previous accounts have been superseded by the researches of Troebst.

5 *Kaempfer's enlistment in the Dutch East India Company*

1 See Meier-Lemgo, *Biographie*, p.15; see above, p.6.
2 'Sed praevaluit suasu Reverendi senis, Patris du Mans [...] invitatio architalassi Batavorum.' *Amoenitates exoticae*, p.[xiv].
3 *Geschichte und Beschreibung von Japan*, vol.I, p.lxiii. Meier-Lemogo, *Biographie*, pp.55ff.
4 Meier-Lemgo, *Biographie*, p.14; for a contrary view, Hoppe, *Gesellschaft*, p.135f.
5 *Amoenitates exoticae*, p.[xiv]. See Meier-Lemgo, *Biographie*, p.55. See above, note 2.
6 On this, see Schuster-Walser, p.88f.
7 This circumstance was partly his own fault, however, as he suggested to van Heuvel that he should initially employ him not on a permanent basis but for a trial period. See the letter of 3.9.1684, Sloane 3063, 127v ff. *Briefe*, p.13.
8 *Reisetagebücher*, p.102.
9 ibid., p.97f.
10 ibid., p.99f.
11 Thus, with regard to Naqsh-i Rustam, he criticises the representations of Thévenot and Hyde. *Amoenitates exoticae*, p.317f.
12 The illustrations published in Chardin's work on Persia (*Journal du voiage du Chevalier Chardine en Perse & aux Indes Orientales* [...], first edition 1688, later issued in many different languages) were also attacked in this work by De Bruijn, who had himself visited Persepolis. With the express purpose of criticising Kaempfer and Chardin he published the *Aenmerkingen*. On this, see Drijvers, pp.76-9. Even if De Bruijn does at one point take the errors of the engraver into account (*Aenmerkingen*, p.40), his critique still seems rather polemical in view of the brief duration of Kaempfer's sojourn on the spot.
13 On this, see Homayoun, pp.179ff.
14 For an evaluation of Chardin, Kaempfer and De Bruijn see Homayoun, p.183f. It is worth remarking, nor is it irrelevant in assessing Kaempfer's achievement, that the illustrations in the *Amoenitates exoticae* were substantially inferior to Kaempfer's drawings – a circumstance that his contemporaries were, of course, unable to appreciate. The background, in terms of the history of ideas and culture, has now been thoroughly dealt with by Wiesehöfer; on the circumstances referred to here, see ibid., p.132 and figs.1, 2, 4 and 5, among others.
15 On this see Beck, *Ritter*, pp.117-20. See also note 9 to ch.12, below.
16 On this problem, see also the essay by Schmeißer, who discusses the changes in the delineation of the drawings and the consequences of these for the representation on the basis of the illustrations in the *History of Japan* as well as in the *Geschichte und Beschreibung von Japan* and of the preparatory sketches for these. He also provides an introduction to the iconographic history of some motifs.
17 *Amoenitates exoticae*, p.335; quoted here from *Reisetagebücher*, p.98.
18 Niebuhr, vol.2, p.149.
19 *Amoenitates exoticae*, p.332, here quoted from Ceram, p.200. The slab copied by Kaempfer was last illustrated by Drijvers, p.66.
20 'Inscriptionem exhibet, expressam characteribus peregrinis, formam habentibus

cuneolorum', *Amoenitates exoticae*, p.331.

21 On the history of the deciphering of cuneiform and Kaempfer's role in it, see Doblhofer, pp.92-130.

22 One of the most recent contributions to the comparison of the different copies and drawings is that of Drijvers.

23 On this see Flaskamp, *Westfälische Geschichte*, p.178. On the reception of Hafiz and Sa'di, see Flaskamp, ibid. Decisive for the history of their influence in Europe, however, was not the translation by Hammer-Purgstall but the earlier translation by Olearius in 1654. See Olearius, ed. by Dieter Lohmeier, p.67*, no.19.

24 *Reisetagebücher*, p.125f.

25 He wrote, inter alia: 'This climate is harmful to my health, my life, my nature. I suffer constant attacks. I have had dropsy for two months [...]. Barely had I escaped this evil, when I fell victim to another in June. I had a violent fever, which is called Maligna tertiana duplex.' *Briefe*, p.19.

26 That is its title in the manuscript. See Sloane 2910, fol.128-38.

27 *Phoenix persicus*, p.62; *Amoenitates exoticae*, p.665.

28 *Phoenix persicus*, pp.31ff.

29 ibid., p.41.

30 ibid., pp.152-6.

31 ibid., p.161f. Kaempfer errs in assuming that it was a swarm of locusts rather than quails.

32 In contrast, say, to Georg Meister, who in his work *Der orientalisch-indianische Kunst- und Lust-Gaertner* does not take that step but keeps his botanical descriptions separate from the regional, historical and linguistic information, thus depriving them of much of their intrinsic liveliness.

33 On Humboldt's aims, see Beck, *Dioskuren*, pp.126-82; here especially pp.127ff.

34 On asafoetida, see Royle & Headland; on Persian bitumen, Schmitz & Meier-Lemgo.

35 *Amoenitates exoticae*, pp.436-54; in compiling this relation Kaempfer made use of a treatise by Fr Raphael.

36 *Amoenitates exoticae*, pp.509-15. Kaempfer appears to be the first to associate the shocks emitted by the fish with electricity. See Walker in: Carruba & Bowers, *Torpedo fish*, p.265.

37 *Amoenitates exoticae*, pp.524-35.

38 Apart from della Valle, the following works concerning Persia were in his library: Jean Chardin, *Persian- und ostindische Reisebeschreibung*, Leipzig, 1687 (*Catalogus*, p.28, no.54); Tavernier's *Reizen*, pt.2, Amsterdam, 1682 (ibid., p.35, no.170).

39 In Sloane 2908. In addition he received from Fr du Mans ten sheets 'Du nom et origine des Chrestiens de St Jean'. Sloane 3063. Sloane 2912 contains, inter alia, extracts from the journals of the Dutch East India Company envoy Joan Cunaeus and Carel Reuierse (from 1651/52) as well as of Huibert de Lairesse (from 1666). Sloane 2920 contains, inter alia, excerpts from Jean Chardin's *Couronement de Soleiman troisième* (1671) as well as from della Valle and Chardin. A number of the Sloane files contain memoranda on history and natural history, vocabularies, notes on Persian and Turkish grammar as well as botanical drawings. They con-

tain also the travel diaries. On the holdings of the British Museum (now the British Library), see Bonn, especially pp.87-99.

40 e.g. in the letter to Parvé of 1.11.1702. See Sloane 3063, 50r ff. *Briefe*, p.44, wrongly dated.

41 The work by Thomas Hyde for which Kaempfer asked in 1701 (Sloane 3036, 51v; *Briefe*, p.44), *Historia religionis veterum Persarum*, remained in his library. See *Catalogus*, p.31, no.109.

42 *Amoenitates exoticae*, p.[xvi]; quoted here from *Seltsames Asien*, p.9.

43 *Amoenitates exoticae*, p.[xii].

44 Sloane 3064, fol.15r-16v; here fol.15r. 'Zoo dat ik niet anders kan voorzien, of Zÿn L. zal van daar een rÿken oegst te ruch brengen, die Zÿn L^s naam door gantsch Europa zeer roem-ruchtigh t'æternizeren heeft.' (23.6.1690.)

45 'Alterum, culpæ chalcographorum quorundam tribuo, quos nactus fui rudes & morosi ingenii; imagines enim meâ manu accuratè & ad typum, sed diversâ magnitudine, delineatas, dum in decentem formam, ex majori vel minori reducere debebant, ita deformârunt, ut, nisi ad illustrandas res omnino essent necessariæ, eas, velut libri dedecus, repudiarem. Atque hæc causa est, cur sextum fasciculum, videlicet epistolarum mearum ad viros in Asiâ eruditos, planè omittam; disserunt enim de iis rebus, quæ sine iconibus, accuratâ manu & me præsente ex sculpendis, non intelliguntur.' *Amoenitates exoticae*, preface, p.[xvii]f.

46 Hüls, *Spuren*, p.171.

47 ibid.

48 *Reisetagebücher*, p.144.

49 ibid.

50 Kaempfer's description of Muscat and his drawings are the best things from this period. On this, see Weisgerber, p.99.

51 On the position of the Coromandel and Malabar coasts, Bengal and the adjoining regions in the commercial policy of the Company's empire, see Gaastra, pp.16-19.

52 *Amoenitates exoticae*, pp.454-66. On the significance of Kaempfer's account see Carrubba, *Ordeal by fire*, p.106.

53 *Amoenitates exoticae*, pp.557-60 and 561-4. See Berger & Hesse on the accuracy of Kaempfer's description.

54 *Reisetagebücher*, p.152.

55 Sloane 3036, fol.61r; *Briefe*, p.16.

56 Letter to Fr Raphael of October 1689, Sloane 3063, fol.65v; *Briefe*, p.25.

57 For a correction to the route, see *Reisetagebücher*, p.158. Kaempfer writes: 'in [...] regionem Sinus Gangetici concedo. Deinde secundum littora Summatrae in Javam deportatus.' *Amoenitates exoticae*, p.[xiv]. This statement must be due to a lapse of memory; it is hardly likely that ships of the Dutch East India Company made such enormous detours. [This is debatable: the Latin text probably means that he 'left the region of the Bay of Bengal', i.e. the Coromandel Coast, and not literally the delta of the Ganges. (Transl.)]

58 It was not published until 1741-55 but was almost completed by 1689, when Kaempfer reached Java. On Rumpf see Biller, in Whittle, p.331f. See also Gaastra, p.202f.

59 Herbert de Jager (1636/37-94) studied theology, mathematics, botany and astronomy. From 1662 onward he was a clergyman and teacher in the service of the Company (in Java, Persia, on the Coromandel Coast, at Batavia, and again in 1683-7 in Persia, where he got to know Kaempfer). See *Nieuw Nederlandsch Biographisch Woordenboek*, Leiden, vol.VII, col.654.

60 Andreas Cleyer (ca.1634-1697/98) was employed by the Company as a soldier, became headmaster of the grammar school in Batavia and during 1682-3 and 1685-6 chief merchant (*opperhoofd*) at Deshima, from which he was banished from smuggling. In Batavia he became a member of the supreme court and laid out botanical gardens at his own expense. See Steenis, p.110.

61 Letter to Nicolaas Witsen in the summer of 1691. Sloane 3063, fol.84v. *Briefe*, p.30.

62 See Kraft, p.55 and p.58, note 114.

63 ibid.

6 The voyage to Siam and Japan

1 Meier-Lemgo, *Biographie*, p.109.
2 On the history of the Christian mission, see Boxer and Cary.
3 See the work of Georg Meister.
4 A source superior to many others is Bernhard Varen (Varenius), who produced a kind of summary of information about Japan in his *Descriptio regni Japoniae* (Amsterdam, 1649; new edition Darmstadt, 1974).
5 'The most important Asian supplier of precious metals for the VOC was Japan. From the counting-house at Deshima large quantities of 'barge silver' were exported until 1668, followed by a change-over from silver to the golden kobangs necessitated by the export ban. During the years 1640-9 Deshima dispatched silver to the value of not less than 15 million guilders, while about 3 million were exported from Persia […]. […] The enormous profits at Deshima were, however, reduced when the Japanese authorities in 1671 adopted a policy of unilaterally fixing the prices of all imported goods'. Gaastra, p.47.
6 Details of the voyage from *Geschichte und Beschreibung von Japan*, vol.I, pp.4ff.
7 On this, see Bodart-Bailey, *Kaempfer*, p.155f. See also the short essay by Frankfurter, which deals only with Kaempfer's language studies in Thailand. His linguistic observations may be compared to those of Imai. On Kaempfer's observations in Siam and their significance for Thai studies, see the extensive and critical assessment in: Terwiel, *Thai history*; Terwiel, *Journal*; Terwiel & Sternstein, *Prospects*.
8 A summary account is provided by Pauly.
9 *Geschichte und Beschreibung von Japan*, vol.I, p.73.

7 Kaempfer's stay at Deshima and his journeys to Edo

1 An initial view of the contemporary European literature on Japan is provided by the *Bibliographischer Alt-Japan-Katalog 1542-1853*. Beyond that, the two-volume

collection of texts *Japan in Europa*, edited by Peter Kapitza, offers an excellent survey of European knowledge of Japan during that period.

2 For instance François Caron (ca.1600–73), who was chief merchant in Japan in the service of the Dutch East India Company from 1621, with brief interruptions, until 1641. On the basis of his experiences he wrote the *Beschrijvinghe van het machtigh coninckrijcke Japan* (Amsterdam, 1648), which subsequently also appeared in other European languages.

3 e.g. that of Georg Meister.

4 e.g. the few pages in Christoph Frick's *Ost-Indianische Reisen und Krieges-Dienste [...]* from the eighties of the seventeenth century. Now in Kapitza, vol.1, pp.934-8, and Laures.

5 For instance Andersen, Mercklein, Langhanss and Vogel. See H. von Schulz, pp.44-56 and 64-78; Kreiner, pp.6-14.

6 Varenius, pp.197ff., contains a list of the works he used.

7 On this, see the detailed survey by Kreiner, *Deutschland – Japan*, pp.1-28.

8 One of the most common themes was the inspection of the ships. The proud and martial attitude of the Japanese, their willingness to learn and the modesty and beauty of their women were likewise objects of European interest. The commerce is also, of course, frequently referred to.

9 Osterhammel, *Reisen*, p.236. There is still no comprehensive textual analysis of the travel accounts of the seventeenth and eighteenth centuries, which would enable us to arrive at a real understanding of how European perceptions of Asian cultures evolved. Osterhammel's expression that 'one [moved] through cultural landscapes that may already have been understood superficially but were largely undeciphered at a deeper level' is a casually formulated admission of precisely this problem of definition, which did not apply equally to all geographical areas and periods. A Raphael du Mans or a Tavernier knew Persia better – and Kaempfer, Meister, Schamberger and Cleyer probably had a more accurate conception of Japan – than many other travellers. See ibid., p.251. On the visual aesthetics of exotic regions and the problem of their perception in Europe, see in addition Kopplin, pp.318-45, and for the basic theory Pochat.

10 On this, see Fujikawa, pp.48ff., and *Red-hair medicine*, in particular also Michel, *Moxa-Spiegel*; Michel, *Medizin*; Michel, *ten Rhijne* (I); Michel, *ten Rhijne* (II).

11 *Geschichte und Beschreibung von Japan*, vol.I, p.lxvi.

12 ibid., p.lxvii.

13 ibid. On his identity, see Brown, *Legacy*, pp.346-51, and Van de Velde, passim.

14 See also the works of the missionaries Frois, Solier and Crasset.

15 *Amoenitates exoticae*, pp.478ff.

16 *Geschichte und Beschreibung von Japan*, vol.II, pp.394-414.

17 The young Dohm deserves credit for the mere fact that he commented at length on the treatise. However, his critique unmistakably reveals his ignorance of Japanese culture as well as his nationally conditioned Enlightenment outlook. Free trade, unhindered access to every part of the world, the overthrow of 'tyranny' – these are all elements of the belief in progress during the last quarter of the eighteenth century. Dohm pays it the sincerest tribute when he writes: 'never will it [the Japanese nation] advance in the culture and enlightenment to which it so

perversely denies access; never will it extend the range of its pleasures, never increase and refine its productions to the extent that would otherwise be possible; never, finally, can it hope for foreign assistance against the despotism that so violently oppresses it.' *Geschichte und Beschreibung von Japan*, vol.II, p.422. On the different reactions in Europe to the seclusion of Japan, see Kreiner, p.32f.

18 e.g. on the origins of the Japanese and the position of the emperor and shogun. Thus both he and Thunberg were mistaken in the presumed extent of hill terracing, which is particularly common around the bay of Nagasaki but not in the rest of the country. See Rein, vol.2, p.23.

19 See Olearius, ed. by Dieter Lohmeier, pp.49*-56*.

20 See Michel, *Schamberger* (I).

21 *Geschichte und Beschreibung von Japan*, vol.II, p.178.

22 ibid., p.186f.

23 *Geschichte und Beschreibung von Japan*, vol.II, p.149.

24 The dates and the route of the journey are taken from the *Geschichte und Beschreibung von Japan*, vol.II, pp.198ff.

25 Apart from his secret notes, Kaempfer had obtained official guides and town plans, which provided him with basic material for his book. See Bonn, pp.99ff.

26 Kaempfer refers also to the fact that the chief merchant, at a second audience, had to listen to the regulations and promise to follow them, but he makes no mention of this in his notes on the visit to Edo. See *Geschichte und Beschreibung von Japan*, vol.II, pp.275-90; esp. p.281f.

27 ibid., p.281.

28 ibid., p.282.

29 ibid., p.285f. Kaempfer sings the song once more during the mission a year later, when the Dutch are again obliged to provide such performances. See ibid., p.352f.

30 *Geschichte und Beschreibung von Japan*, vol.II, p.285f.

31 Appropriately enough he apostrophises his 'old flame' Florimene as one who had been faithful, not as one who still remained faithful; Meier-Lemgo, *Biographie*, p.141.

32 On the original, see Bonn, p.107, referring to a coloured town plan of Edo from the year 1681 among the Japanese books and maps of Kaempfer's acquired by Sloane. Plate XXX (*Geschichte und Beschreibung von Japan*, vol.II, opposite p.270) is correctly described as: 'Ichnographia Urbis IEDO [...] ex Mappa Japonica Musei Sloaniani.'

33 They were described primarily by de Bondt (1657), Cleyer (1683) and ten Rhijne (1683). Kaempfer first dealt with them in chapters IX and X of his dissertation (see *Disputatio medica*) and then in a revised form in part III, sections 11 and 12, of the *Amoenitates exoticae*.

34 *Geschichte und Beschreibung von Japan*, vol.III, p.435.

35 ibid., plate opposite p.438.

36 See Michel, *Moxa-Spiegel*, pp.212ff.; Michel, *Medizin*, pp.281-5.

37 He writes in a footnote: 'I feel that Kaempfer falls into the same error here on which I have already remarked in relation to the previous dissertation, namely to elevate the procedures and customs of the foreign country above those of our own.' *Geschichte und Beschreibung von Japan*, vol.II, p.424.

38 On this topic in the history of medicine, see Michel, *Beobachtungen*. He has also produced a model biography of Caspar Schamberger, who worked as a barber-surgeon in Japan. See Michel, *Schamberger* (II)-(V).

39 See Sloane 74 and Sloane 2914; *Amoenitates exoticae*, p.[xiii].

40 Of the plants on which Kaempfer brought information to Europe the best-known is probably the ginkgo tree. It is not actually native to Japan but to China, yet more than almost any other plant it has become a symbol of the Far East and especially of Japan. Apart from his thorough account of the value represented by the multiple uses of its fruits and seeds, Kaempfer established the characteristic form of its name. See Widder, Thommen.

41 On this see Michel, *ten Rhijne* (I) and *ten Rhijne* (II); Michel, *Sendschreiben*.

42 Teleki, p.154.

43 See Teleki, whose work is still of fundamental importance for the cartography of Japan. Also Campbell and, most recently, Walter; on the problem of the Gyoki maps, see Cortazzi, p.23f.

44 See also the maps of Reland and Chatelain, especially the influence of the so-called Gyoki maps on the distribution of provinces and their names.

45 See Bonn, pp.104-7.

46 *Geschichte und Beschreibung von Japan*, vol.I, following p.lxviii. On this, see Lazar, *Kaempfer*, p.275f., and Lazar, *Kartographf*.

47 Seutter's and Tirion's maps of 1730 and 1735 still adopt the erroneous notion of a connection between Hokkaido and Kamchatka. Vaugondy (1750) and Bellin (1752, and later) are also, in their delineation, heirs of Kaempfer. Through new editions of their maps this image of Japan continued to be accepted throughout the eighteenth century.

8 *Homeward voyage from Asia*

1 Letter to Lycochthon, Sloane 3063, fol.94rff.

2 Sloane 3063, fol.81v; *Geschichte und Beschreibung von Japan*, vol.I, p.xxvii.

3 Sloane 3063, fol.92r.

4 See Meier-Lemgo, *Biographie*, pp.145, 162.

5 Sloane 3063, fol.78r.

6 *Geschichte und Beschreibung von Japan*, vol.II, p.382.

7 Petition of 23.1.1693 to the Governor General of the Company, Willem van Outhoorn, *Briefe*, p.33.

8 See the muster roll of the *Pampus* in Sloane 3064, fol.40v. It is interesting to note that, among 118 employees, it placed Kaempfer in fourth position after the captain (70 guilders), first officer (65 guilders) and ship's surgeon (48 guilders).

9 *Briefe*, p.34. Though Kaempfer still had an active desire for achievement, it does seem somewhat rash to conclude: 'Thus at one point Kaempfer seriously, if briefly, entertained a daring plan – having already explored a large part of Asia – to tackle southern Africa as well!' Meier-Lemgo, *Biographie*, p.164. Who is to say that he was not also influenced by the pleasant climate and the environment, which were obviously charming in human as well as topographical terms?

9 Conferment of doctorate and return to Lemgo

1 The following exposition is based on the exhaustive research on this subject in Hüls, *Promotion*.
2 *Briefe*, p.36. Kaempfer later revised his dissertation again and published its chapters in a different sequence and in an expanded form in the *Amoenitates exoticae*. On this, see Hüls, *Promotion*, p.188, note 26.
3 Among these are his opinion on the origin of the fleece of 'Scythian lamb'. See Bowers & Carrubba, *Doctoral thesis*, p.277, note 18, as well as Lee, p.24, and most recently Kämpfer, p.83f. His opinion about the therapeutic effect of Persian mummy is probably secondhand. See Bowers & Carrubba, *Doctoral thesis*, p.283, note 9.
4 On the significance of Kaempfer's description see Carrubba & Bowers, *Torpedo fish*.
5 His description of Madura foot, for instance, not only provides an account of the pathology that remains largely valid even today but is also a significant example of communication between West and East. See Berger & Hesse, p.183f.
6 See Arnold, pp.24ff. The charge of 'excessive enthusiasm' that he levels at Kaempfer (ibid., p.26) can be traced back to Dohm (*Geschichte und Beschreibung von Japan*, vol.II, p.424f.). It is, however, understandable (and in no way attributable to any deficiency in Kaempfer's critical faculties) if one bears in mind the surgical practices in Europe at that time (on which see Diepgen, vol.I, pp.317ff.). In that respect it is irrelevant how much was known about Chinese and Japanese medicine.
7 *Geschichte und Beschreibung von Japan*, vol.II, pp.423-61.
8 Hüls unfortunately provides no detailed information about this, presumably for lack of sources. Hüls, *Promotion*, p.186.
9 Letter of 22.4.1694. *Briefe*, p.37.
10 See *Stammbuch*, p.193.

10 Last years in Lieme

1 Sauerländer, p.145f.
2 The '*formula juramenti*', i.e. the oath of service, is preserved in the Staatsarchiv Detmold (L 16 B Nr2).
3 Only two letters are actually preserved, addressed to a certain nobleman, Jean Frid[rich?] von Bückeburg (Sloane 3063, fol.38r f. and 41v; it has not been possible to identify this correspondent so far), but in view of the paucity of documents for this period it is unlikely that Kaempfer only wrote these two letters with advice and prescriptions. It may safely be assumed that the major part of Kaempfer's correspondence has been lost or destroyed.
4 See e.g. the letter of 20 April 1702; 'sometimes friends came to rob me of my time, sometimes the crowd of invalids'. *Briefe*, p.44.
5 Among these was the General, Count Ferdinand Christian zur Lippe, who stayed 'for a couple of hours'. See Kittel, *Memoiren*, p.91.
6 *Briefe*, p.41f. On the intended effect of this letter see Meier-Lemgo, *Biographie*,

p.172, who describes Kaempfer's frame of mind quite well. How little Meier-Lemgo, nevertheless, understands Kaempfer as a man of the Baroque is revealed by his remark that one cannot 'brush aside' the 'painful impression' 'that this intelligent and moral man viewed his marriage principally as a financial matter'. Ibid. That, however, together with the aim of ordering one's life, is precisely what it was until well into the century, before other values such as personal happiness came to the fore.

7 Schwanold, pp.57ff.
8 ibid., p.47.
9 ibid.
10 ibid., p.46.
11 ibid.
12 ibid.
13 ibid.
14 ibid., p.53. The clearest evidence of Maria Sophia's attitude is her marriage to Dr Johnn Hermann Capelle on 28 August 1717 – still within the year of mourning!
15 ibid., p.56f.
16 Though one surely cannot speak of an 'ardent love' for his sister Anna Catherina, his relationship with her seems to have been affectionate and trusting. See Hoppe, *Gesellschaft*, p.145f.
17 'Eng. Kämpfer earned particular merit with regard to the ecclesiastical autonomy of Lieme.' Butterweck, p.489. On Kaempfer's commitment, see above p.ooof.
18 See Meier-Lemgo, *Biographie*, p.175f.
19 They were reprinted again in the second edition of this work (ed. Johann Conrad Becker). Ibid., pp.489-93.
20 Lüders, in Haccius, p.54.
21 ibid., p.56. Lüders also provides a fairly detailed account of the final months. Ibid., pp.54ff. For an analysis of the funeral sermon in the context of studies of biographical literature, see Lenz, pp.56-8.

11 The reception of Kaempfer in the eighteenth and nineteenth centuries

1 A detailed account of him is given by MacGregor.
2 On the sale of Kaempfer's papers, see Bonn, pp.76-86; most recently again, exhaustively and precisely, Massarella. Although in essence he comes to the same conclusions as Bonn (cf. ibid., p.11, note 4), he does describe the role of Zollman more accurately; unless new documents come to light it is unlikely that anything further can be added to the facts established by Massarella.
3 Bonn, pp.76-81; Massarella, p.17f.
4 It is worth nothing that a change of title occurred so early. The title chosen by Kaempfer naturally reflected his own intentions much better, as it correctly emphasised the actuality rather than the compendiousness suggested later by his editor.
5 Meier-Lemgo, *Biographie*, p.186.
6 Hüls, *Bibliographie*, no.265.

7 ibid., nos.273, 274, 275. Around 1740 an atlas volume was also added (no.276).

8 ibid., nos.234, 235.

9 On the bibliographic history see Hüls, *Druck*, p.193.

10 In his *Nachricht die Urschrift der Kämpferschen Beschreibung von Japan betreffend* (Lemgo, 1774) as well as in the preface to the work he provides a detailed justification for his editorial procedure. He compares the autograph manuscript, Johann Hermann's copy and Scheuchzer's translation and produces a linguistically modernised version: 'I therefore adopted the following rule: to preserve the sense and ideas of Kaempfer with the greatest conscientiousness and minute accuracy, neither adding nor subtracting anything, while at the same time presenting these unmodified ideas in as readable a form and as polished a style as possible without doing any injury to the historical truth.' *Geschichte und Beschreibung von Japan*, vol.I, p.xlii. With due regard to Dohm's achievement, the problematic aspect of his procedure emerges here: Dohm, strongly influenced by the Enlightenment and the spirit of Diderot, produced a version that did indeed appeal to the German reading public of his time but obscured the baroque character of the work. This is more than just a matter of style, as every modernisation of an historic text causes the loss of idiosyncrasies of the author, his scientific outlook and much else besides.

11 Sloane 2914.

12 On this see Dawson's edition of Banks's letters. A reprint of the *Icones* is included in the set of the *Geschichte und Beschreibung von Japan* (OAG).

13 The following may be mentioned here: Car von Linné, *Potus Theae*. In: *Amoenitates Academicae*, vol.VII, diss. 137. Holmiae, 1765; Carl Peter Thunberg, *Flora Iaponica*, deals with Kaempfer primarily in his own travel account. See Hüls, *Bibliographie*, nos.448, 449.

14 In the article 'Japonais, Philosophie des'. It states, inter alia, that: 'Le célebre Kempfer qui a parcouru le Japon en naturaliste, géographe, politique & théologien, & dont le voyage tient un rang distingué parmi nos meilleurs livres, divise l'histoire *japonoise* en fabuleuse, incertaine & vraie.' [D'Alembert & Diderot:] *Encyclopédie*, t.8, pp.455-8; here p.455.

15 On this see Kapitza, *Aufklärung*.

16 Ritter, *Geographie*, pt.4, bk.2: Asien, vol.3, p.1145.

17 ibid., pt.9, bk.3: West-Asien, p.746. Ritter spoke from knowledge, as he had carefully read and evaluated Kaempfer's work. See also chapter 12, note 9.

18 On this see Hüls, *Bibliographie*, e.g. nos.380, 387b, 412, 433, 444, 450, 451, 452, 495, 496, 545, 566, 594. It may be of interest, as well as suggestive in terms of the history of his influence, to look at the number of titles (based on Hüls' bibliography). Works on botany amount to 14 in the seventeenth and eighteenth centuries, 20 in the nineteenth and 46 in the twentieth century; on travel the figures are 4, 26 and 103 titles, on medicine 3, 1 and 28, and on the *Geschichte und Beschreibung von Japan* 7, 1 and 17.

19 Siebold's remark concerning his description of the Moxa is representative of the general recognition of Kaempfer even during the nineteenth century: 'His treatise [...] would deserve to be printed in full here had it not already been reproduced in various books and several languages.' Siebold, vol.2, p.84. Even at the

end of the century Rein's account of travels includes a detailed analysis of his work and the observations contained in it.

20 This is exemplified as late as 1860 by Wilhelm Heine, who includes a 156-page long extract from the *Geschichte und Beschreibung von Japan* in his *Japan und seine Bewohner.*

12 Karl Meier-Lemgo and Kaempfer studies in the twentieth century

1 On whom see *Karl Meier-Lemgo 100 Jahre*; Beck, *Gedächtnis*, pp.5-8; now also Haberland, *Lemgoer Hefte* 3.

2 Meier-Lemgo, *Fahrt.*

3 Unfortunately Meier-Lemgo time and again produced idealised descriptions for which the sources provide no evidence. The fact that Kaempfer was deeply rooted in the seventeenth century was a subject he did not explore. This historically problematic approach gave rise to many faulty assessments and exaggerations.

4 See the list of sources in the bibliography. Bowers, *Rezension*, discusses in detail Meier-Lemgo's editing of the travel diaries.

5 Beck in *Geschichte und Beschreibung von Japan*, vol.I, p.v. On the position of Kaempfer in the history of travel see the same author's *Große Reisende*, p.8of.

6 *Geschichte und Beschreibung von Japan*. OAG.

7 Johann Casper Scheuchzer: 'Nachricht so wol von dieser als auch von andern das Japonesische Reich betreffenden Beschreibungen' (1727/1749); Peter Kapitza: 'Engelbert Kaempfer und die europäische Aufklärung. Zur Wirkungsgeschichte seines Japanwerks im 18. Jahrhundert'; the same 'Biographische Notiz' [on Kaempfer]; Hans Hüls: 'Zur Geschichte des Drucks von Kaempfers Geschichte und Beschreibung von Japan und zur sozioökonomischen Struktur von Kaempfers Lesepublikum im 18. Jahrhundert'; Tadashi Imai: 'Anmerkungen zu Engelbert Kaempfers Geschichte und Beschreibung von Japan. Ein japanologischer Kommentar.' The last two contributions were republished two years later in *Engelbert Kaempfer zum 330. Geburtstag.*

8 Translation of and commentary on the *Valedictio* and the medical dissertation by Rohtraut Müller-König & Hans Hüls; Tadashi Imai: 'Kaempfer und seine Quellen'; Imai: 'Sprachliche und landeskundliche Anmerkungen zu Engelbert Kaempfers Geschichte und Beschreibung von Japan'; Hans Hoppe: 'Die diplomatischen Missionen des schwedischen Gesandten Ludwig Fabritius in Moskau und Isfahan gegen Ende des 17 Jahrhunderts'; Hans Hüls: 'Auf den Spuren Engelbert Kaempfers in Iran'; Hüls: 'Engelbert Kaempfers Promotion in Leiden 1693/1694'; Hüls: 'Zur Geschichte des Drucks von Kaempfers "Geschichte und Beschreibung von Japan" und zur sozioökonomischen Struktur von Kaempfers Lesepublikum im 18. Jahrhundert'; Hüls: 'Internationale Kaempfer-Bibliographie'.

9 Not listed, though informative on its reception in the eighteenth and nineteenth centuries, is August Hennings's critical discussion of Kaempfer's work (1786). Although included in Kapitza, the reference to the *Encyclopédie* of D'Alembert & Diderot should not have been omitted (see chapter 11, note 14). Hüls has failed

to note the numerous references to Kaempfer in Carl Ritter (Ritter, *Erdkunde*, pt.4, bk.2: pp.1078, 1079, 1083f., 1086, 1089, 1093, 1098, 1099, 1102, 1106, 1110, 1113, 1128, 1133, 1134, 1138, 1145, 1155, 1192, 1209ff.; pt.9, bk.3: pp.737, 739, 741, 743, 744, 746, 751, 753, 823, 827, 835, 850, 851, 856, 857, 930, 933, 935). This demonstrates Kaempfer's exceptional value as a source for Ritter. Likewise, Johann Justus Rein (*Japan nach Reisen und Studien*) not infrequently draws on Kaempfer: vol.1, p.365f.; vol.2: pp.23, 42, 58, 66, 102, 135, 141, 169, 172, 183, 349, 463, 468, 596, 622f., 624. He is cited also as an informant on Persepolis and the cuneiform script in one of the most important encyclopaedias of the nineteenth century, Ersch/Gruber (vol.14, p.378; vol.17, p.349; vol.32, p.242; vol.35, p.100a). Also of interest is the listing of the various auction sales of Scheuchzer's *History of Japan*; see Lowndes, p.1252 (vol.2).

10 On this, see the review by Walravens.

11 This text, too, is published without the original Latin, which reduces its value as a source. On this, as well as on some liberties taken in translation, see the review by Goltz.

12 Terwiel, *Thai history*.

13 Muntschick, *Georg Meister*; Michel, 'Georg Meister' (the scope of the latter essay extends far beyond the field of botany).

14 Bodart-Bailey, *Kaempfer*, pp.152-5; see also her *Kaempfer restor'd*.

15 Bodart-Bailey, *Preliminary report*.

16 'Kaempfer's album of famous sights of seventeenth century Japan.' Two years later Bodart-Bailey also wrote on this subject, without adding anything significant; on a topic such as this repeated research appears rather unproductive. See Bodart-Bailey, *Most Magnificent Monastery*.

17 See Beck, *Erdwissenschaftliche Erschließung Japans*; Beck, *Germania in Pacifico*.

18 It is a pity that the concepts of a 'journey of exploration' and 'explorer' are again applied to Kaempfer in this work and determine its line of argument. Hoppe, *Kaempfers Reisen*, p.8.

19 Unfortunately vol.4 appeared in 1983, too early for Boxer to include the more recent literature.

20 Brenner, pp.134-40. 'What is still lacking is an examination of the work [on Japan] that defines its place in the generic history of travel accounts and provides a thorough analysis and interpretation of the text.' Ibid., p.139.

21 The volume brings together studies by Harm Klüting, Nagazumi Yôko, K. Elke Werger-Klein and Wolfgang Muntschick on general issues of scientific and biographical history; by Frank Kämpfer, Jan Willem Drijvers, Josef Wiesehöfer, Albertine Gaur, Barend J. Terwiel and Larry Sternstein on Russian, Persian, Indian and Siamese themes; by Paul van der Velde, Wolfgang Michel, Wolfgang Muntschick and Jörg Schmeisser on problems concerning Kaempfer's work on Japan; by Herbert Bräutigam, Yu-Ying Brown, Margarete Lazar, Larry Sternstein, Barend J. Terwiel and Detlef Haberland on aspects of the work relating to cartography, reception studies and textual criticism.

22 In this regard an influence that requires no further elaboration may be perceived from the research on the early modern period which has expanded significantly during the last thirty years.

23 This applies not only to Kaempfer, of course; Leibniz or Kircher might be mentioned here as outstanding examples.

24 During the last few years this unsatisfactory state of things has been repeatedly addressed. Thus the writer referred to the current situation as early as 1989 in a lecture given in Lemgo on the history and future development of Kaempfer studies. See also Haberland, *Kaempfer*, p.323; Terwiel, *Thai history*, p.79. Bodart-Bailey subscribes to this opinion in regard to the work on Japan. See Bodart-Bailey, *Kaempfer restor'd*, pp.14ff. However much one welcomes her plan for a new translation of the work on Japan into English, priority must be given to the genesis of the original German text and its relative significance in terms of the history of science. On the evaluation of authentic texts and their importance for an historical-critical edition Scheibe, p.28f., is still worth consulting. Further research has failed to establish any significantly different principles since then. Muntschick, *Nachlese*, presents a contrary view regarding a new edition of Kaempfer's texts.

25 Kapitza already referred to this in his 'Biographische Notiz' in the volume of commentary on the *Geschichte und Beschreibung von Japan*, OAG, p.166f.

26 The second edition of Meier-Lemgo's *Biographie* is based on the edition of 1937 and was by no means thoroughly revised and adapted to the state of research but merely improved in a few minor aspects.

27 See the many references on p.71 of the supplementary volume to that work.

28 Landwehr, no.265 (p.121), no.266 (p.125), nos.529-34 (pp.305-14), no.616 (p.383), no.619 (p.384), no.639 (p.402).

29 Kreiner, *Kenperu*. The volume brings together the following contributions: Detlef Haberland, Eva Kraft and Josef Kreiner on the life of Kaempfer, on relations between Japan and Europe and on Cleyer and Meister as predecessors of his; Harm Klüting, Moriya Takeshi, Nagazumi Yôko, Oishi Shinsaburô and Sakurai Tetsuo on the economy, society and music of the Genroku period as well as the persecutuion of witches in the Age of Faith and on the relations between Japan and the Netherlands; Eberhard Friese and Haga Tôru on Kaempfer as an exponent of comparative cultural history; on recent trends in Kaempfer studies, on the Kaempfer material in the British Library, on the material he brought back viewed from an ethnographic perspective, on the 'views of famous places' and, finally, on Kaempfer and his interpreter Imamura Gen'emon: Yu-Ying Brown, Katagiri Kazuo, Josef Kreiner, Matsuda Kiyoshi, Naka Naomichi, Nagazumi Yôko, Hans Dieter Ölschleger, Sakakibara Satoru and Tashio Kazui.

30 See Michel, *Beobachtungen*; Michel, *Japans Rolle*. His studies on Caspar Schamberger (I-V) also deal with this topic. On the basis of a letter from Cleyer to Scheffer he establishes the background, involving German scholars in the service of the Company in East Asia. See his *Sendschreiben*.

31 In particular the exclusive citing of Dohm's edition and the lack of references should be critically noted; the indication that Massey intends to write a monograph on Kaempfer (Massey, *Kroniekschrijver*, p.136) allows one to suppose that she will confront the various problems at a more fundamental level.

32 Unsatisfactory (though in themselves justifiable) are general articles like that of Hornstein in the *Lexikon der Reise- und Abenteuerliteratur* (1993), which abounds

in factual mistakes and errors of assessment and where the biographical references are arbitrary, incomplete and wrong.

33 See Haberland, *Lemgoer Hefte* 1-4.
34 Haberland, *Wunderkammer*, p.93.
35 Lenz, pp.56-8.
36 Terwiel, *Manuscript collections*.
37 Haberland, *Critical edition*.
38 See Bodart-Bailey, *Kenperu*. Parts of the book had already been published elsewhere by Bodart-Bailey; overall, it neither adds anything new to the research on Kaempfer nor resolves any fundamental questions. In the bibliography (pp.248-50) she does not take account of recent research; though that does not diminish the readability of the book for a wider public, it can therefore hardly be regarded as a synthesis of the research on Kaempfer during the last ten years.
39 London: Curzon Press, 1996.
40 'Forgotten practices of the past: Kaempfer's strange description of the Japan emperor.' Using Kaempfer's portrayal of the Japanese emperor as an example, she very knowledgeably shows the sources from which it was drawn and how it was received in Europe.
41 'Inquisitive and intelligent men.' Massarella is able to give a clear account, based on numerous references, of the reasons for Sloane's interest in Kaempfer. In comparison with Thomas Hyde it becomes apparent how much Kaempfer differed, through his empirical endeavours, from other armchair scholars and thereby actually opened a door to the future. Essays such as this can give the reader a graphic idea of the circumstances of 'academic life' in the pre-Enlightenment era.
42 'Writing the *History of Japan*.' The English title, provided by Sloane or Scheuchzer, actually blurs the topical relevance that Kaempfer himself saw in his work, which he therefore gave the title (Sloane 3060): *Heutiges Japan. Zu einer Zweifachen Hoff-reise durchgeschauet und beschrieben etc.* This is not the place to discuss the change of title, significant as it is for the history of geographical theory.

13 The way ahead

1 Meier-Lemgo, *Reisetagebücher*, pp.1-3; he already recognised the basic problem: 'We do not know, to be sure, whether other notes have been lost [...].' Ibid., p.3. This assessment has now been proved correct by the work done on the letters and the *Amoenitates*.
2 On this, see *Texte und Varianten*; Kraft, *Editionsphilologie*.
3 The plan for an edition provisionally envisages the following arrangement of volumes (subject to the commentary, which can hardly be estimated in advance): vol.1, *Amoenitates exoticae*, with the *Disputatio medica*, in five parts; vol.2, *Heutiges Japan*, in five parts; vol.3, *Noticiae indicae*; vol.4, travel diaries; vol.5, cartography; vol.6, letters; vol.7, botany, in three parts; vol.8, linguistics; vol.9, music; vol.10, *Exercitatio politica* and the album amicorum; vol.11, extracts and excerpts; vol.12, varia (Kaempfer's collections and library).
4 The publishing side of the whole project will be handled by the Iudicium-Verlag in Munich; the overall publisher will be assisted by an international scientific

advisory panel. In this connection it should also be recorded that the preliminary work and production of a draft, the printing contract, the appointment of a number of volume editors as well as the reproduction of all of Kaempfer's approximately 1300 drawings is being promoted by the Land of North Rhine-Westphalia, the town of Lemgo, the British Library and its contributors, the British Council and the German Academic Exchange Service as well as the publishing company itself, whose chief executive Dr Peter Kapitza is providing energetic and committed support for the project.

5 Thus it will have to be positively demonstrated (and can be demonstrated only through the editing process!) whether Kaempfer, as some have asserted, can claim the status of a philosopher in his own right or what significance should be attributed to his linguistic studies, which have so far hardly been evaluated. On the aims of the edition and the suppositions on which it is based, see also Haberland, *Werkstattbericht*.

6 Falkmann, p.63; on the justification for this epithet, see Haberland, *Wunderkammer*, p.93.

Bibliography

Only the works that have been used for this biography are listed below, with no attempt to provide a full Kaempfer bibliography; the reader will find copious information from the periods covered respectively by the bibliographies of Hüls (Hüls, *Bibliographie*) and the conference volume *Engelbert Kaempfer: Werk und Wirkung*, pp.426-61. Authors' names alone are cited, with distinguishing title words where there are several works by the same author.

Sources

[Engelbert Kaempfer:] *Amoenitatum exoticarum politico-physico-medicarum fasciculi V, quibus continentur variæ relationes, observationes & descriptiones rerum Persicarum et Ulterioris Asiae, multâ attentione, in peregrinationibus per universum Orientem, collectæ,* ab auctore Engelberto Kæmpfero, D. Lemgoviæ, 1712.
Amoenitates exoticae
Engelbert Kaempfer: *Am Hofe des persischen Großkönigs* (1684-5). *Das erste Buch der Amoenitates exoticae.* Eingeleitet u. in deutscher Bearbeitung hrsg. v. Walther Hinz. Leipzig, 1940. *Amoenitates exoticae, ed. by Walther Hinz*
Karl Meier-Lemgo: *Die Briefe Engelbert Kaempfers.* Wiesbaden, 1965. (Akademie der Wissenschaften und der Literatur. Abhandlungen der Mathematisch-naturwissenschaftlichen Klasse. Jahrg.1965, Nr.6.) *Briefe*
Catalogus verschiedener rarer und auserlesener theologisch-juristisch-medicinisch-philosophisch-philologisch- und historischer Buecher welche den 25ten October 1773 und folgende Tage des Morgens um 9 und des Nachmittags um 2 Uhr in Lemgo in der seel. Jungfer Kaempfern Behausung an den Meistbietenden verkauft, jedoch ohne baare Bezahlung in Conventionsmuenze nicht verabfolget werden sollen. Lemgo, 1773. *Catalogus*
Engelbert Kaempfer: 'Disputatio medica inauguralis exhibens decadem observationum exoticarum [...].' Aus dem Lateinischen übersetzt v. Hans Hüls u. Rohtraut Müller-König. In: *Engelbert Kaempfer zum 330. Geburtstag [...].* Lemgo, 1982. pp.31-61. *Disputatio medica*
Engelbert Kaempfer: 'Exercitatio politica de majestatis divisione in realem et personalem [...].' Aus dem Lateinischen übertragen v. Rohtraut Müller-König. In: *Engelbert Kaempfer zum 330. Geburtstag [...].* Lemgo, 1982. pp.15-29.
Exercitatio
Engelbert Kaempfer: *Flora japonica* (1712). Reprint des Originals und Kommentar v. Wolfgang Muntschick. Wiesbaden, 1983. *Flora japonica*
Engelbert Kaempfer: *Geschichte und Beschreibung von Japan.* Aus den Originalhandschriften des Verfassers hrsg. v. Christian Wilhelm Dohm. Unveränderter Neudruck des 1777-9 im Verlag der Meyerschen Buchhandlung in Lemgo

erschienen Originalwerks. Mit einer Einführung von Hanno Beck. 2 vols. Stuttgart, 1964. (Quellen und Forschungen zur Geschichte der Geographie und der Reisen. Bd.2.)   *Geschichte und Beschreibung von Japan*
Engelbert Kaempfer: *Geschichte und Beschreibung von Japan*. Aus den Originalhandschriften des Verfassers. hrsg. v. Christian Wilhelm Dohm. Lemgo 1777-9. Hrsg. im Auftrag der OAG, Tokyo. Berlin, Heidelberg, New York, 1980. [With a facsimile reprint of the *Icones selectae plantarum, quas in Japonia collegit et delineavit Engelbertus Kaempfer; ex archetypis in Museo Britannico asservatis*, London 1791; including a volume containing *Beiträge und Kommentar*].
    Geschichte und Beschreibung von Japan, OAG
Engelbert Kaempfer: *The History of Japan: Giving an Account of the ancient and present State and Government of that Empire; of its Temples, Palaces, Castles, and other Buildings; of its Metals, Minerals, Trees, Plants, Animals, Birds and Fishes; of the Chronology and Succession of the Emperors, Ecclesiastical and Secular; of the Original Descent, Religions, Customs, and Manufactures of the Natives, and of their Trade and Commerce with the Dutch and Chinese; together with a Description of the Kingdom of Siam*. Written in High Dutch by Engelbertus Kæmpfer, M.D. Physician to the Dutch Embassy to the Emperor's Court; and translated from his Original Manuscript, never before printed, by J. G. Scheuchzer, F.R.S. and a Member of the College of Physicians, London. With the Life of the Author and an Introduction. Illustrated with many Copper Plates. 2 vols. London, 1727.   *The History of Japan*
Engelbert Kaempfer: *Phoenix persicus: die Geschichte der Dattelpalme*. Einleitung, Übersetzung aus dem Lateinischen u. Bearbeitung v. Wolfgang Muntschick. Marburg, 1987.   *Phoenix persicus*
Die Reisetagebücher Engelbert Kaempfers. Bearbeitet v. Karl Meier-Lemgo. Wiesbaden, 1968. (Erdwissenschaftliche Forschung. Bd.II).   *Reisetagebücher*
Engelbert Kämpfer: Seltsames Asien <Amoentiates exoticae>. In Auswahl übersetzt von Karl Meier-Lemgo. Detmold, 1933.   *Seltsames Asien*
Karl Meier-Lemgo: Das Stammbuch Engelbert Kämpfers. In: *Lippische Mitteilungen aus Geschichte und Landeskunde*, Bd.21 (1952), pp.142-200.   *Stammbuch*

Secondary literature

[D'Alembert & Diderot:] *Encyclopédie, ou Dictionnaire raisonné des sciences, des arts et des métiers [...]*. Tome 8ème. Neufchastel, 1775 (Reprint 1967).
Arnold, Hans-Jürgen: *Die Geschichte der Akupunktur in Deutschland*. Heidelberg, 1976.
[Baur, Gustav Adolf Ludwig:] 'Andreas Kempffers Selbstbiographie nach der Giessener Handschrift zum erstenmal hrsg., eingeleitet u. erl.' In: [*Programm*] *zur Feier des Reformationsfestes und des Übergangs des Rectorats auf D. Christoph Ernst Luthardt [...]*. Leipzig, 1880.
Beck, Hanno: 'Alexander von Humboldt als größter Geograph der Neuzeit.' In: *Die Dioskuren: Probleme in Leben und Werk der Brüder Humboldt*. Abhandlungen v. Hanno Beck [et al.]. Hrsg. v. Herbert Kessler. Mannheim, 1986. pp.126-82.

(Abhandlungen der Humboldt-Gesellschaft für Wissenschaft, Kunst und Bildung, Bd.9). *Beck, Dioskuren*

Beck, Hanno: *Geschichte der erdwissenschaftlichen Erschließung Japans.* Probevorlesung gehalten am 13.2.1963 vor der Mathematisch-Naturwissenschaftlichen Fakultät der Rheinischen Friedrich-Wilhelms-Universität zu Bonn. [Manuscript]. *Beck, Erdwissenschaftliche Erschließung Japans*

Beck, Hanno: 'Europa und Japan: zur Begegnung zweier Kulturen von 1295 bis zur Gegenwart.' In: *Reiseberichte als Quellen europäischer Kulturgeschichte.* Aufgaben und Möglichkeiten der historischen Reiseforschung. Hrsg. v. Antoni Maczak u. Hans Jürgen Teuteberg. Wolfenbüttel, 1982. (Wolfenbütteler Forschungen, Bd.21). *Beck, Europa*

Beck, Hanno: 'Dem Gedächtnis von Prof. Dr. Karl Meier-Lemgo.' In: *Lippische Mitteilungen aus Geschichte und Landeskunde*, Bd.8 (1969), pp.5-8. [With a bibliography of the works of Meier-Lemgo by Erich Kittel, pp.8-16.]
Beck, Gedächtnis

Beck, Hanno: *Geographie: Europäische Entwicklung in Texten und Erläuterungen.* Freiburg, München, 1973. (Orbis academicus, Bd.II/16.) *Beck, Geographie*

Beck, Hanno: *Germania in Pacifico: der deutsche Anteil an der Erschließung des Pazifischen Beckens.* Wiesbaden, 1970. (Akademie der Wissenschaften und der Literatur. Abhandlungen der Mathematisch-naturwissenschaftlichen Klasse, Jahrg.1970, Nr.3). *Beck, Germania in Pacifico*

Beck, Hanno: 'Die Geschichte der Reisen: Grundzüge und Perspektiven eines Teilgebietes der Historie der Geographie.' In: *Praxis Geographie*, Jahrg.18 (1989), Hft.3 (März), pp.6-10. *Beck, Geschichte*

Beck, Hanno: *Große Reisende: Entdecker und Erforscher unserer Welt.* München, 1971.
Beck, Große Reisende

Beck, Hanno: 'Carl Ritters Darstellung der "iranischen Welt" oder wie Europa einstmals ein großes Land geographisch kennenlernte.' In: *Iranzamin: Echo der iranischen Kultur*, Jahrg.2 (1983), Ausgabe 1(7), pp.117-20. *Beck, Ritter*

Beer, Johann: *Die teutschen Winter-Nächte & kurzweiligen Sommer-Täge.* Zwei Romane (1682/83). Hrsg. u. mit einem Nachwort, Anmerkungen u. Worterklärungen versehen v. Richard Alewyn. Frankfurt a.M., 1985.

Berger, Hermann & Klaus Hesse: 'Die Beschreibung des Madurafußes durch Engelbert Kämpfer (1651-1716).' In: *Der Hautarzt: Zeitschrift für Dermatologie, Venerologie und verwandte Gebiete*, Jahrg.20 (1969), Hft.4, pp.182-5.

Bibliographischer Alt-Japan-Katalog 1542-1853. Bearb. u. hrsg. v. Japaninstitut in Berlin u. v. Deutschen Forschungsinstitut in Kyoto. Kyoto, 1940 (Reprint 1977).

Bodart-Bailey, Beatrice M.: 'Kaempfer restor'd.' In: *Monumenta Nipponica*, vol.43, no.1 (Spring 1988), pp.1-33. *Bodart-Bailey, Kaempfer restor'd*

Bodart-Bailey, Beatrice M.: *Kenperu to Tokugawa Tsunayoshi: Doitsu ishi to shōgun tono kōryō* [Kaempfer and Tokugawa Tsunayoshi: the encounters of a German physician with the Shōgun]. Transl. by Naka Naoitsu. Tōkyō, 1994. (Chūō shinsho, no.1168). *Bodart-Bailey, Kenperu*

Bodart-Bailey, B[eatrice] M.: 'Kyoto three hundred years ago.' In: *Nichibunken Newsletter*, no.9 (May 1991), pp.4-12. *Bodart-Bailey, Kyoto*

Bodart-Bailey, Beatrice M.: 'The Most Magnificent Monastery and other famous sights: the Japanese paintings of Engelbert Kaempfer.' In: *Japan Review* 1992, no.3, pp.25-44.   *Bodart-Bailey, Most Magnificent Monastery*

Bodart-Bailey, Beatrice: 'Preliminary report on the manuscripts of Engelbert Kaempfer in the British Library.' In: *Japanese studies: Papers presented at a colloquium at the School of Oriental and African Studies, University of London 14-16 September 1988.* Ed. by Yu-Ying Brown. London, 1990. pp.22-39.

Bodart-Bailey, Preliminary Report

Bodart-Bailey, Beatrice M.: 'Warum noch einmal Kaempfer?' In: *Lippische Mitteilungen aus Geschichte und Landeskunde,* Bd.57 (1988), pp.149-67.

Bodart-Bailey, Kaempfer

Bodart-Bailey, Beatrice M. & Derek Massarella: *The Furthest Goal. Engelbert Kaempfer's Encounter with Tokugawa Japan.* London, 1996.

Bonn, Gerhard: 'Der wissenschaftliche Nachlaß des lippischen Forschungsreisenden Engelbert Kaempfer im Britischen Museum.' In: *Lippische Mitteilungen aus Geschichte und Landeskunde,* Bd.48 (1979), pp.69-116.

Bowers, John Z. & Robert W. Carrubba: 'The doctoral thesis of Engelbert Kaempfer on tropical diseases, Oriental medicine, and exotic natural phaenomena.' In: *Journal of the History of Medicine and Allied Sciences,* vol.XXV (1970), no.3, pp.270-310.   *Bowers & Carrubba, Doctoral Thesis*

Bowers, John Z.: [Review of Meier-Lemgo's edition of Kaempfer's travel diaries (1968).] In: *Erasmus: Speculum scientiarum,* vol.21 (1969), no.9/10 (10 May 1969), col.315-17.   *Bowers, Rezension*

Boxer, Charles R.: *The Christian century in Japan 1549-1650.* Berkeley, 1951.

Boxer, C[harles] R.: [Article 'Kaempfer, Engelbert'.] In: *Kodansha Encyclopedia of Japan.* Tokyo, 1983. Vol.4, p.101f.

Braubach, Max: *Vom Westfälischen Frieden bis zur Französischen Revolution.* 8. Aufl. München, 1988. (Gebhardt, Handbuch der deutschen Geschichte, Bd.10.)

Brenner, Peter J.: *Der Reisebericht in der deutschen Literatur: ein Forschungsüberblick als Vorstudie zu einer Gattungsgeschichte.* Tübingen, 1990. (Internationales Archiv für Sozialgeschichte der deutschen Literatur. Sonderheft 2).

Brown, Yu-Ying: 'Daiei Toshokan shozo Kenperu shorai Nihon shiryo no igi.' In: *Doitsujin no mita Genroku jidai – Kenperu ten.* Tokyo, 1990. pp.101-110.

Brown, Daiei Toshokan

Brown, Yu-Ying: 'Engelbert Kaempfer's legacy in the British Library.' In: *Engelbert Kaempfer: Werk und Wirkung.* [...]. pp.344-69.   *Brown, Legacy*

Brown, Yu-Ying: 'Japanese books and manuscripts: Sloane's Japanese library and the making of the *History of Japan.*' In: Arthur MacGregor (ed.): *Sir Hans Sloane: collector, scientist, antiquary, founding father of the British Museum.* London, 1994. pp.278-90.   *Brown, Japanese Books*

Brown, Yu-Ying: 'Kaempfer's Album of Famous Sights of Seventeenth Century Japan.' In: *The British Library Journal,* vol.15, no.1 (Spring 1989), pp.90-103.

Brown, Sights

[Bruijn, Cornelis de]: *Aanmerkingen over de Printverbeeldingen van de Overblyfzelen van het Oude Persepolis, Onlangs uitgegeven door de Heeren Chardin en Kempfer, waer in derzelver misteekeningen en gebreken klaer worden aengewezen,* door Cornelis de Bruin. Amsterdam, 1714.   *De Bruijn, Aanmerkingen*

Bruijn, Cornelis de: *Reizen over Moskovie, door Persie en Indie: verrykt met driehond-ert konstplaten, vertoonende de beroemdste lantschappen en steden, ook de byzondere dragten, beesten, gewassen en planten, die daer gevonden worden: voor al derzelver oudheten en wel voornamentlyk heel uitvoerig, die van heerlyke en van oudts de geheele werrelt door befaemde hof van Persepolis, by de Persianen Tchilminar genaemt.* Amsterdam, 1711.   *De Bruijn, Reizen over Moscovie*

Butterweck, W[ilhelm]: *Die Geschichte der lippischen Landeskirche.* Schötmar, 1926.

Caesar, Wolfgang: 'Ginsengwurzel in Europa. Eine alte Geschichte.' In: *Deutsche Apotheker Zeitung,* Jahrg.131 (1991), Nr.19 (9. Mai), pp.935-41.

Campbell, Tony: *Japan: Printed maps to 1800.* London, 1967. (Map Collector's Circle, no.36).

Carrubba, Robert W. & John Z. Bowers: 'Engelbert Kaempfer's first report of the torpedo fish of the Persian Gulf in the late seventeenth century.' In: *Journal of the History of Biology,* vol.15, no.2 (Summer 1982), pp.263-74.
Carrubba & Bowers, Torpedo fish

Carrubba, Robert W.: 'Kaempfer's Latin account of the ordeal by fire in Siam.' In: *Acta orientalia,* Bd.XLVI (1985), pp.101-9.   *Carrubba, Ordeal by Fire*

Carrubba, Robert W.: 'Pastor H. G. Weland's Latin elegy for Engelbert Kaempfer.' In: *Gesnerus: Swiss Journal of the History of Medicine and Sciences,* vol.51 (1994), pt.1/2, pp.34-44.   *Carrubba, Pastor*

Cary, Otis: *A history of Christianity in Japan: Roman Catholic, Greek Orthodox, and Protestant missions.* Rutland, 1976.

Ceram, C. W.: *Götter, Gräber und Gelehrte im Bild.* Hamburg, 1957.

Christliche Leich-Predigt/ bey der sehr volck-reichen und hoch-ansehnlichen Leich-Begängniß des weyland Hoch-Edlen/ Vesten und Hochgelahrten Herrn Hn. Joachimi Kaempffers [...] von Julio Friedrich Lueder [...]. Lemgo, 1710.
Leich-Predigt Joachim Kaempffer

Conze, Werner: [Article 'Monarchie']. In: *Geschichtliche Grundbegriffe: Historisches Lexikon zur politisch-sozialen Sprache in Deutschland.* Hrsg. v. Otto Brunner, Werner Conze, Reinhart Koselleck. Bd.4. Stuttgart, 1978. pp.168-89.

Cortazzi, Hugh: *Isles of Gold: antique maps of Japan.* New York, Tokyo, 1983.

[Crasset, R. P. J.:] *Histoire de l'Eglise du Japon.* Par le R. P. J. Crasset, de la Compagnie de Jesus. 2 vols. Seconde éd. Paris, 1691.

Dahlgren, E. W.: *Les débuts de la cartographie du Japon.* Uppsala, 1911 (Reprint 1977).

Dawson, Warren R.: *The Banks letters: a calendar of the manuscript correspondence of Sir Joseph Banks preserved in the British Museum (Natural History) and other collections in Great Britain.* London, 1958.

Diepgen, Paul: *Geschichte der Medizin: die historische Entwicklung der Heilkunde und des ärztlichen Lebens.* Bd.1: Von den Anfängen der Medizin bis zur Mitte des 18. Jahrhunderts. Berlin, 1949.

Doblhofer, Ernst: *Zeichen und Wunder: die Entzifferung verschollener Schriften und Sprachen.* Wien, Berlin, Stuttgart, 1957.

Drijvers, Jan Willem: ' "Deez tekende en schreef niet anders dan hij zag": Cornelis de Bruijn, Nicolaes Witsen en Gysbert Cuper.' In: *Persepolis en Pasargadae in wisselend perspectief: Iraanse oudheden beschreven en getekend door Europese reizigers.* Samengesteld door Heleen Sancisi-Weerdenburg. In: *Phoenix*, vol.35, 1 (1989), pp.63-80.

Emblemata: Handbuch zur Sinnbildkunst des XVI. und XVII. Jahrhunderts. Hrsg. v. Arthur Henkel u. Albrecht Schöne. Stuttgart, 1967.

Engelbert Kaempfer: Werk und Wirkung: Vorträge der Symposien in Lemgo (19.-22.9.1990) und in Tokyo (15.-18.12.1990). Hrsg. v. Detlef Haberland im Auftrag der Engelbert-Kämpfer-Gesellschaft (Lemgo) und des Deutschen Instituts für Japanstudien (Tokyo). Stuttgart, 1992. (Boethius, Bd.32).

Engelbert Kaempfer zum 330: Geburtstag: Gesammelte Beiträge zur Engelbert-Kaempfer-Forschung und zur Frühzeit der Asienforschung in Europa. Zusammengestellt u. bearbeitet v. Hans Hüls u. Hans Hoppe. Hrsg. in Verbindung mit der Engelbert-Kämpfer-Gesellschaft Lemgo e.V. Deutsch-Japanischer Freundeskreis. Lemgo, 1982. (Lippische Studien. Bd.9).

[Erler, Georg:] *Die Matrikel der Albertus-Universität zu Königsberg i.Pr. 1544-1829.* Bd.II: Die Immatrikulationen von 1657-1829. Hrsg. v. Georg Erler. Leipzig, 1911-12 (Reprint 1976).

Ersch, J. S. and J. G. Gruber (eds.): *Allgemeine Encyclopaedie der Wissenschaften und Kuenste in alphabetischer Folge von genannten Schriftstellern.* Sekt. 1-3. Leipzig, 1818-89.   *Ersch/Gruber*

Estreicher, Karol: *Collegium Maius: Stammsitz der Jagellonischen Universität Krakau: Geschichte, Bräuche, Sammlungen.* Warschau, 1974.

Falkmann, [August]: 'Kämpfer, Engelbert.' In: *Allgemeine deutsche Biographie*, Bd.15 (1882), pp.62-4.

Flaskamp, Franz: 'Engelbert Kemper: Persien, Indien und Japan in frühestdeutscher Sicht.' In: *Archiv für Kulturgeschichte*, Bd.48 (1966), Hft.1, pp.84-113.
Flaskamp, Persien

Flaskamp, Franz: 'Herders Bücherkauf zu Lemgo: ein Beitrag zur Geschichte der Bibliotheca Herderiana.' In: *Jahrbuch der Gesellschaft für Niedersächsische Kirchengeschichte*, Bd.65 (1967), pp.218-35.   *Flaskamp, Bücherkauf*

Flaskamp, Franz: 'Quellen, Ergebnisse und Aufgaben der Kemper-Forschung.' In: *Forschungen und Fortschritte*, Jahrg.41 (1967), Hft.6, pp.171-4.
Flaskamp, Quellen

Flaskamp, Franz: 'Am Ostufer der Bibel: Engelbert Kempers medische Reise.' In: *F. F.: Westfälische Geschichte in 50 Einzeluntersuchungen.* Gütersloh, 1968. pp.175-8.   *Flaskamp, Westfälische Geschichte*

Frankfurter, O.: 'Some remarks on Kaempfer's description of Siam, 1690.' In: *Journal of the Siam Society*, vol.VI (1909), pt.3, pp.22-31.

Franz, Walther: *Geschichte der Stadt Königsberg.* München, 1934. (Ostpreußische Landeskunde in Einzeldarstellungen.) [Reprint 1979].

[Frois, Luis:] *Die Geschichte Japans (1549-1578).* Von Luis Frois S. J. Nach der Ajudabibliothek in Lissabon übersetzt und kommentiert v. G. Schurhammer u. E. A. Voretzsch. Leipzig, 1926.

Fujikawa, Y.: *Geschichte der Medizin in Japan: Kurzgefasste Darstellung der Entwicklung der japanischen Medizin mit besonderer Berücksichtigung der europäischen Heilkunde in Japan.* Tokyo, 1911.

Fürstenwald, Maria (ed.): *Trauerreden des Barock.* Wiesbaden, 1973. (Beiträge zur

Literatur des XV. bis XVIII. Jahrhunderts, Bd.IV).

Gaastra, Femme S.: 'Die Vereinigte Ostindische Compagnie der Niederlande – ein Abriß ihrer Geschichte.' In: Eberhard Schmitt, Thomas Schleich, Thomas Beck (eds.): *Kaufleute als Kolonialherren: die Handelswelt der Niederländer vom Kap der Guten Hoffnung bis Nagasaki 1600-1800.* Bamberg, 1988. pp.1-89. (Schriften der Universitätsbibliothek Bamberg, Bd.6).

Gabriel, Alfons: *Die Erforschung Persiens: die Entwicklung der abendländischen Kenntnis der Geographie Persiens.* Wien, 1952.

Gaul, Otto and Ulf-Dietrich Korn: *Stadt Lemgo.* Stadtgeschichtliche Einleitung v. Hans Hoppe. Münster, 1983. (Bau- und Kunstdenkmäler von Westfalen, Bd.49, Tl.1).

Gause, Fritz: *Die Geschichte der Stadt Königsberg in Preußen.* Bd.I: Von der Gründung der Stadt bis zum letzten Kurfürsten. Köln, Graz, 1965.

Goltz, Dietlinde: [Review of *Phoenix Persicus*, see Sources.] In: *Gesnerus: Swiss Journal of the History of Medicine and Sciences*, vol.45 (1988), pt.1, p.149f.

Haberland, Detlef: 'Nulli peregrinatorum secundus: the critical edition of the printed and unpublished works of Engelbert Kaempfer.' In: *IIAS* [International Institute for Asian Studies] *Newsletter*, no.3 (Autumn 1994), p.56f.
Haberland, Critical Edition

Haberland, Detlef: 'Engelbert Kaempfer: Leben – Werk – Wirkung.' In: *800 Jahre Lemgo: Aspekte der Stadtgeschichte.* Hrsg. v. Peter Johanek u. Herbert Stöwer. Lemgo, 1990. pp.311-25. *Haberland, Kaempfer*

Haberland, Detlef: 'Engelbert Kaempfer: Arzt, Reisender und "Entdecker" Japans.' In: *Kulturvermittler zwischen Japan und Deutschland: Biographische Skizzen aus vier Jahrhunderten.* Hrsg. v. Japanischen Kulturinstitut Köln. Frankfurt a.M., New York, [1990]. pp.9-30. *Haberland, Kulturvermittler*

Haberland, Detlef: 'Engelbert Kaempfer – ein Reise- und Gelehrtenleben im 17. Jahrhundert. Tl.1: Von Lemgo nach Asien.' In: *Lemgoer Hefte*, Hft.2 (April 1995), p.20-4. *Haberland, Lemgoer Hefte 1*

Haberland, Detlef: 'Engelbert Kaempfer – ein Reise- und Gelehrtenleben im 17. Jahrhundert. Tl.2: Von Dejima nach Europa. Letzte Jahre in Lemgo.' In: *Lemgoer Hefte*, Hft.3 (Juli 1995), pp.7-11. *Haberland, Lemgoer Hefte 2*

Haberland, Detlef: 'Engelbert Kaempfer – ein Reise- und Gelehrtenleben im 17. Jahrhundert. Tl.3: Karl Meier-Lemgo. Ein Gelehrtenleben für Kaempfer und die Alte Hansestadt.' In: *Lemgoer Hefte*, Hft.4 (Dezember 1995), pp.3-7.
Haberland, Lemgoer Hefte 3

Haberland, Detlef: 'Engelbert Kaempfer – Ein Reise- und Gelehrtenleben im 17. Jahrhundert. Tl.4: Aspekte der neueren Kaempfer-Forschung.' In: *Lemgoer Hefte*, Hft.2 (Mai 1996), pp.26-30. *Haberland, Lemgoer Hefte 4*

Haberland, Detlef: 'Die kritische Ausgabe der gedruckten und ungedruckten Werke Engelbert Kaempfers: ein Werkstattbericht.' In: *Wolfenbütteler Barock-Nachrichten*, Jahrg 21, Hft.2 (November 1994), pp.134-8.
Haberland, Werkstattbericht

Haberland, Detlef: *Von Lemgo nach Japan: Das ungewöhnliche Leben des Engelbert Kaempfer 1651 bis 1716.* Bielefeld, 1990. *Haberland, Kaempfers Leben*

Haberland, Detlef: 'Zwischen Wunderkammer und Forschungsbericht – Engelbert

Kaempfers Beitrag zum europäischen Japanbild.' In: *Japan und Europa 1543-1929*. Hrsg. von Doris Croissant und Lothar Ledderose [Katalog der Berliner Festspiele]. Berlin, [1993]. pp.83-93.   *Haberland, Wunderkammer*

[Haccius, Johann Berthold:] *Die beste Reise eines christlichen Kaempffers nach dem himmlichen Orient. Nach Anleitung der Worte in I. Timoth. VI. v. 12. Bey hochansehnlicher Leich-Bestattung des weyland Hoch-Edlen/ Hochgelahrten und Hocherfahrenen Herrn/ ENGELBERT KÆMPFERS, weitberühmten Doctoris Medicinæ, Hoch-Graeflich-Lippischen hoch-betraueten viel-jaehrigen Leib-Medici, und Erbsassen zum Steinhofe bey Lime etc. Als derselbe am 2 Novembr. des 1716 Jahrs in glaubigem Vertrauen auf das Verdienst Christi zum Steinhofe seligst verstorben/ und darauf am 15 solches Monats/ Dominica 23. post Trinit. dessen entseelter Leichnam in der Christ-Evangelischen Haupt-Kirchen zu S. Nicolai in Lemgo Christ-gebuehrlichst zur Ruhe in der Erden versetzet wurde: bey volckreicher christlichen Versamlung in einer Traur- und Gedaechtniß-Predigt/ gelehret und angewiesen/ von JOHANN. BERTHOLD. HACCIUS., V.D.M und Pastore daselbst*. Lemgo, n.d. [1716].

Hartmann, Karl: *Polen*. Nürnberg, 1966.

Heine, Wilhelm: *Japan und seine Bewohner: Geschichtliche Rückblicke und ethnographische Schilderungen von Land und Leuten*. Leipzig, 1860.

Hemann, Friedrich Wilhelm: 'Lemgos Handel und der hansische Verband in Spätmittelalter und Frühneuzeit.' In: *800 Jahre Lemgo: Aspekte der Stadtgeschichte*. Hrsg. v. Peter Johanek u. Herbert Stöwer. Lemgo, 1990. pp.189-238.

Hennings, August: *Gegenwaertiger Zustand der Besitzungen der Europaeer in Ostindien durch A.H. Thl.3: Versuch einer Ostindischen Litteratur-Geschichte nebst einer kritischen Beurtheilung der Aechtheit der Zend-Buecher v. A. H.* Hamburg, Kiel, 1786.

Heuer, Reinhold: *Thorn*. Berlin, 1931. (Deutsche Lande/Deutsche Kunst).

Holsten, Nils von: *Bilder aus der Geschichte der Universität Uppsala*. Uppsala, 1936. (Uppsala Universitets årsskrift, 1936, hft.5).

Homayoun, Gholamali: *Iran in europäischen Bildzeugnissen vom Ausgang des Mittelalters bis ins 18. Jahrhundert*. Diss. [Typescript.] Köln, 1967.

Hoppe, Hans: 'Die diplomatischen Missionen des schwedischen Gesandten Ludwig Fabritius in Moskau und Isfahan gegen Ende des 17. Jahrhunderts.' In: *Engelbert Kaempfer zum 330. Geburtstag [...]*. Lemgo, 1982. pp.155-66.
                                                                                     Hoppe, Missione

Hoppe, Hans: 'Engelbert Kaempfers Stellung in der Gesellschaft seiner Zeit. Anhang: Kaempfers Testament.' In: *Engelbert Kaempfer zum 330. Geburtstag [...]*. Lemgo, 1982. pp.133-54.   *Hoppe, Gesellschaft*

Hoppe, Hans: 'Engelbert Kaempfers Reisen zu Wasser und zu Lande.' In: *Engelbert-Kämpfer-Gymnasium Lemgo 1583-1983*. Lemgo, 1983.
                                                                                Hoppe, Kaempfers Reisen

Hornstein, Elisabeth von: 'Engelbert Kaempfer (Deutschland) 1651-1716.' In: Friedrich Schegk (ed.): *Lexikon der Reise- und Abenteuerliteratur*. Meitingen. Suppl. 21 (Dezember 1993), pp.1-14, 1-4.

Hüls, Hans: 'Auf den Spuren Engelbert Kaempfers im Iran.' In: *Engelbert Kaempfer zum 330. Geburtstag [...]*. Lemgo, 1982. pp.167-82.   *Hüls, Spuren*

Hüls, Hans: 'Engelbert Kaempfers Promotion in Leiden 1693/1694.' In: *Engelbert Kaempfer zum 330. Geburtstag [...]*. Lemgo, 1982. pp.183-90.
Hüls, Promotion

Hüls, Hans: 'Internationale Kaempfer-Bibliographie.' In: *Engelbert Kaempfer zum 330. Geburtstag [...]*. Lemgo, 1982. pp.209-58.
Hüls, Bibliographie

Hüls, Hans: 'Zur Geschichte des Drucks von Kaempfers "Geschichte und Beschreibung von Japan" und zur sozialökonomischen Struktur von Kaempfers Lesepublikum im 18. Jahrhundert.' In: *Engelbert Kaempfer zum 330. Geburtstag [...]*. Lemgo, 1982. pp.191-208.
Hüls, Druck

Imai, Tadashi: 'Sprachliche und landeskundliche Anmerkungen zu Engelbert Kaempfers Geschichte und Beschreibung von Japan.' In: *Engelbert Kaempfer zum 330. Geburtstag [...]*. Lemgo, 1982. pp.83-132.

Japan und Europa 1543-1929. Eine Ausstellung der '43. Berliner Festwochen' im Martin-Gropius-Bau Berlin. Hrsg. v. Doris Croissant, Lothar Ledderose unter Mitwirkung v. Hendrik Budde u. Gereon Sievernich. Berlin, 1993.

Jöcher, Christian Gottlieb: *Allgemeines Gelehrten=Lexicon [...]*. 4 vols. Suppl. vol.7. Leipzig, 1750-1897 (Reprint 1960).

Kämpfer, Frank: 'Engelbert Kaempfers "Diarium Itineris ad Aulam Muscoviticam indique Astracanum" und sein Verhältnis zur Moskowitischen und Persianischen Reise von Adam Olearius.' In: *Engelbert Kaempfer: Werk und Wirkung [...]*. Stuttgart, 1992. pp.72-84.

Kapitza, Peter: 'Engelbert Kaempfer und die europäische Aufklärung: zur Wirkungsgeschichte seines Japanwerks im 18. Jahrhundert.' In: *Engelbert Kaempfers Geschichte und Beschreibung von Japan: Beiträge und Kommentar*. In: *Engelbert Kaempfer: Geschichte und Beschreibung von Japan*. Hrsg. v. der Deutschen Gesellschaft für Natur- und Völkerkunde Ostasiens (OAG), Tokyo. Berlin, Heidelberg, New York, 1980. pp.41-64.
Kapitza, Aufklärung

Kapitza, Peter: *Japan in Europa*. Texte und Bilddokumente zur europäischen Japankenntnis von Marco Polo bis Wilhelm von Humboldt. 2 vols., suppl. vol. München, 1990.
Kapitza, Japan in Europa

Karl Meier-Lemgo: 100 Jahre: Sein Leben, sein Werk, seine Zeichnungen. Bearbeitet v. Imke Tappe u. Ernst Tappe. Lemgo, 1982.
Karl Meier-Lemgo 100 Jahre

Kastrop, Rainer: 'Die Bedeutung des Varenius innerhalb der Entwicklung des geographischen Denkens in Deutschland.' In: Manfred Büttner (ed.): *Zur Entwicklung der Geographie vom Mittelalter bis zu Carl Ritter*. Bd.3. Paderborn [etc.], 1982, pp.79-95.

Kelbert, Heinz: 'Engelbert Kämpfer über die Apscheronsche Triade (Erdgas-Erdöl-Schlammvulkane).' In: *Erdölgeologie: Geschichte und Gegenwart: Beiträge zum IV. DDR-UdSSR-Symposium zur Geschichte der Geologischen Wissenschaften, 29. September – 4. Oktober 1986 in Baku*. Hrsg. v. Eginhard Fabian [et al.]. Berlin, 1989. pp.79-86. (Schriftenreihe für geologische Wissenschaften. Series in Geological Sciences, Hft. 27).

Kittel, Erich: *Geschichte des Landes Lippe: Heimatchronik der Kreise Detmold und Lemgo*. 2. Aufl. Köln, 1978.
Kittel, Geschichte

Kittel, Erich (ed.): *Memoiren des braunschweigisch-lüneburgischen Generals Graf Ferdinand Christian zur Lippe (1668-1724)*. Lemgo, 1959. (Sonderveröffentlichun-

gen des Naturwissenschaftlichen und Historischen Vereins für das Land Lippe.
Bd.XII).   *Kittel, Memoiren*

Kleinwegener, Günter: *Die Hexenprozesse von Lemgo*. Diss. [Typescript.] Bonn,
1954.

Klimaszewski, Boleslaw (ed.): *An outline of the history of Polish culture*. Krakau, 1979.

Kopplin, Monika: '"Amoenitates exoticae": Exotische Köstlichkeiten im Zeitalter
des Barock.' In: *Exotische Welten: Europäische Phantasien: Katalog*. Stuttgart,
1987. pp.318-45.

Kraft, Eva (ed.): 'Andreas Cleyer: Tagebuch des Kontors zu Nagasaki auf der Insel
Deshima. 20. Oktober 1682 - 5. November 1683.' In: *Bonner Zeitschrift für
Japanologie*, Bd.6 (1985).

Kraft, Herbert: *Editionsphilologie*. Mit Beiträgen von Jürgen Gregolin, Wilhelm Ott
u. Gert Vonhoff. Darmstadt, 1990.   *Kraft, Editionsphilologie*

Krause, Johann Gottlieb: *Nova litteraria eruditorum in gratiam divulgata [...]*.
Leipzig, 1718. pp.63-7.

Kreiner, Josef (ed.): 'Deutschland – Japan: die frühen Jahrhunderte.' In: *Deutschland – Japan: Historische Kontakte*. Bonn, 1984. pp.1-53. (Studium universale,
Bd.3).   *Kreiner, Deutschland – Japan*

Kreiner, Josef (Hrsg.): *Kenperu no mita Tokugawa-Japan [Kaempfer sees the Japan of
the Tokugawa era]*. Tokyo, 1992.   *Kreiner, Kenperu*

Landwehr, John: *VOC: a bibliography of publications relating to the Dutch East India
Company 1602-1800*. Ed. by Peter van der Krogt. Utrecht, 1991.

Laures, Johannes: *Kirishitan Bunko: a manual of books and documents on the early
Christian mission in Japan*. Tokyo, 1957.

Lazar, Margarete: *Engelbert Kaempfer als Kartograph und Geograph*. Diss. [Type-
script.] Wien, 1980.   *Lazar, Kaempfer*

Lazar, Margarete: 'The manuscript maps of Engelbert Kaempfer.' In: *Imago Mundi:
the journal of the International Society for the History of Cartography*, vol.34
(1982), pp.66-71.   *Lazar, Kartograph*

Lee, Henry: *The vegetable lamb of Tartary; a curious fable of the cotton plant: to which
is added a sketch of the history of cotton and the cotton trade*. London, 1887.

Lenz, Rudolf: *De mortuis nil nisi bene? Leichenpredigten als multidisziplinäre Quelle
unter Berücksichtigung der historischen Familienforschung, der Bildungsgeschichte
und der Literaturgeschichte*. Sigmaringen, 1990. (Marburger Personalschriften-
Forschungen, Bd.10).

*Lexicon Capuccinum: Promptuarium historico-bibliographicum Ordinis fratrorum min-
orum Capuccinorum*. Rome, 1951.

[Lindroth, Sten:] [Article 'Rudbeck, Olof'.] In: *Svenska män och kvinnor*. Biografisk
uppslagsbok. Del 6. Stockholm, 1949.

Linné, Carl von: *Amoenitates academicae*, vol.I. Stockholm, 1744.

Linné, Carl von: 'Potus Theae.' In: *Amoenitates Academiae*, vol.VII. Diss.137.
Holmiae [Stockholm], 1765.

Loewenson, Leo: 'Russian documents in the British Museum. II. 17th century – The
manuscripts of Engelbert Kaempfer.' In: *Slavonic and East European Review*,
vol.14 (1935/36), pp.661-9.

Lowndes, W. T.: *The bibliographer's manual of English literature*. Vol.2. London, 1864.

[Lüder, Friederich Wilhelm:] 'Der unsterbliche und unvergaengliche Tugend-Geruch als der weyland Hoch-Edle/ Hochgelahrte und Hocherfahrne Herr Herr Engelbertus Kaempffer/ Medicinae wuerdigster Doctor, Hochgraefl. Lippischer Hochbestallter Leib-Medicus und Erbsasse auf dem Steinhofe bey Lime/ Am 15. Novemb. Anno 1716. unter ansehnlicher Folge zu seiner Ruh-Kammer solte gebracht werden In einer kurtzen Parentation vorgestellet von Wilhelm Friederich Lüder [...].' In: *Haccius*, pp.58-74.

Lunelund, Birgit: 'Engelbert Kämpfer och hans resa genom Finland 1683.' In: *Historisk tidskrift för Finland*, årg.23 (1938), pp.163-76.

MacGregor, Arthur (ed.): *Sir Hans Sloane: collector, scientist, antiquary, founding father of the British Museum*. London, 1994.

Manthey, Franz: *Polnische Kirchengeschichte*. Hildesheim, 1965.

Martens, Gunter & Hans Zeller (ed.): *Texte und Varianten: Probleme ihrer Edition und Interpretation*. München, 1971.

Massarella, Derek: 'The history of a *History*: the purchase and publication of Engelbert Kaempfer's *History of Japan*.' In: *The Transactions of the Asiatic Society of Japan*, 4th series, vol.8 (1993), pp.9-43.

Massey, Margot: 'Kaempfer alive! Occident in the Orient.' In: *Current Therapy*, vol.4 (1986), no.10, pp.103-6; no.11, pp.155-8; no.12, pp.146-9.
Massey, Kaempfer alive!

Massey, Margot: 'Engelbert Kaempfer (1651-1716): Kroniekschrijver van de Edo-periode.' In: *VOC en cultuur, wetenschapenlijke en culturels relaties tussen Europa en Azie ten tijde van de VOC*. Hrsg. v. J. Bethlehem u. A. C. Meijer. Amsterdam, 1993.
Massey, Kroniekschrijver

Meier-Lemgo, Karl: 'Meine Fahrt nach Engelbert Kämpfers unveröffentlichten Handschriften.' In: *Lippische Post*, Jahrg.82 (1929), Nr.168, 174 (20., 27. Juli).
Meier-Lemgo, Fahrt

Meier-Lemgo, Karl: 'Engelbert Kämpfer als Mann des Willens und der Tat. Ansprache zur Engelbert-Kämpfer-Ehrung 1938.' In: *Der Westfälische Erzieher*. Gauamtliche Halbmonatsschrift des N.S.L.B. Gau Westfalen-Nord. Jahrg.6 (1938), Hft.14 (18. Oktober), pp.328-31.
Meier-Lemgo, Mann des Willens

Meier-Lemgo, Karl: 'Aus Engelbert Kaempfers Leben und Forschung.' In: *Lippische Mitteilungen aus Geschichte und Landeskunde*, Bd.26 (1957), pp.264-76.
Meier-Lemgo, Leben

Meier-Lemgo, Karl: *Engelbert Kämpfer (1651-1716) erforscht das seltsame Asien*. 2. berichtigte u. erw. Aufl. Hamburg, 1960.
Meier-Lemgo, Biographie

Meier-Lemgo, Karl: *Geschichte der Stadt Lemgo*. 2. Aufl. Lemgo, 1962.
Meier-Lemgo, Geschichte

Meister, Georg: *Der Orientalisch-Indianische Kunst- und Lust-Gärtner [...] entworffen und fürgestellet durch George Meistern/ dieser Zeit Churfl. Sächs. bestallten Indianischen Kunst- und Lust-Gärtner [...]*. Dresden, 1692 [Reprint Weimar, 1972].

Michel, Wolfgang: 'Frühe westliche Beobachtungen zur Moxibustion und Akupunktur.' In: *Sudhoffs Archiv für die Geschichte der Medizin und Naturwissenschaften*, Bd.77 (1993), Hft.2, pp.193-222.
Michel, Beobachtungen

Michel, Wolfgang: 'Die Japanisch-Studien des Georg Meister (1653-1713).' In:

Dokufutsu bungaku kenkyu, no.36, Fukuoka, 1986, pp.1-50.

Michel, Georg Meister

Michel, Wolfgang: 'Engelbert Kaempfer und die Medizin in Japan.' In: *Engelbert Kaempfer: Werk und Wirkung [...]*. Stuttgart, 1992. pp.248-93.

Michel, Medizin

Michel, Wolfgang: 'Engelbert Kaempfers merkwürdiger Moxa-Spiegel: Wiederholte Lektüre eines deutschen Reisewerks der Barockzeit.' In: *Dokufutsu bungaku kenkyu*, no.33, Fukuoka, 1986, pp.185-238.　　*Michel, Moxa-Spiegel*

Michel, Wolfgang: 'Wilhelm ten Rhijne und die japanische Medizin (I).' In: *Dokufutsu bungaku kenkyu*, no.39, Fukuoka, 1989, pp.75-126.

Michel, ten Rhijne (I)

Michel, Wolfgang: 'Wilhelm ten Rhijne und die japanische Medizin (II).' In: *Dokufutsu bungaku kenkyu*, no.40, Fukuoka, 1990, pp.57-105.

Michel, ten Rhijne (II)

Michel, Wolfgang: 'Japans Rolle in der frühen Vermittlung der Akupunktur nach Europa.' In: *Deutsche Zeitschrift für Akupunktur. Offizielles Organ der Österreichischen Gesellschaft für Akupunktur und Auriculotherapie. Zeitschrift für die wissenschaftliche Erforschung und praktische Anwendung der Akupunktur in Klinik und Praxis*, Jahrg.36 (1993), Hft.2 (April), pp.40-6.

Michel, Japans Rolle

Michel, Wolfgang, 'Caspar Schambergers "Lebens-Lauff".' In: *Studies in Languages and Cultures*, no.1, Fukuoka, 1990, pp.41-51.　　*Michel, Schamberger (I)*

Michel Wolfgang: 'Caspar Schambergers Kindheit und Jugend.' In: *Dokufutsu bungaku kenkyu*, no.45, Fukuoka, 1995, pp.111-23.　　*Michel, Schamberger (II)*

Michel, Wolfgang: 'Caspar Schambergers Reisen nach Edo.' In: *Dokufutsu bungaku kenkyu*, no.42, Fukuoka, 1992, pp.1-85.　　*Michel, Schamberger (III)*

Michel, Wolfgang: 'Caspar Schambergers Aktivitäten als Barbierchirurg in Japan.' In: *Dokufutsu bungaku kenkyu*, no.44, Fukuoka, 1994, pp.149-86.

Michel, Schamberger (IV)

Michel, Wolfgang: 'Caspar Schamberger (1623-1706): Heimkehr und Leben in Leipzig.' In: *Dokufutsu bungaku kenkyu*, no.43, Fukuoka, 1993, pp.137-95.

Michel, Schamberger (V)

Michel, Wolfgang: 'Ein "Ostindianisches Sendschreiben" – Andreas Cleyers Brief an Sebastian Scheffer vom 20. Dezember 1683.' In: *Dokufutsu bungaku kenkyu*, no.41, Fukuoka, 1991, pp.15-98.　　*Michel, Sendschreiben*

Müller, Kurt: *Gottfried Wilhelm Leibniz und Nicolaas Witsen*. Berlin, 1955. (Sitzungsberichte der Deutschen Akademie der Wissenschaften zu Berlin [Ost]. Klasse f. Philosophie, Geschichte, Staats-, Rechts- u. Wirtschaftswissenschaften. Jahrg.1955, Nr.1).

Muntschick, Wolfgang: 'Ein Manuskript von Georg Meister, dem Kunst- und Lustgärtner, in der British Library.' In: *Medizinhistorisches Journal: Internationale Vierteljahresschrift zur Wissenschaftsgeschichte*, Bd.19 (1984), Hft.3, pp.225-32.

Muntschick, Georg Meister

Muntschick, Wolfgang: 'Nachlese zur Kaempfer-Forschung.' In: *Lippische Mitteilungen aus Geschichte und Landeskunde*, Bd.21 (1985), pp.195-200.

Muntschick, Nachlese

Niceron, [Jean Pierre:] *Memoires pour servir a l'Histoire des Hommes illustres dans la Republique des Lettres: avec un Catalogue raisonne de leurs Ouvrages.* Tome XIX. Paris M.DCC.XXXII.

Niebuhr, Carsten: *Reisebeschreibung nach Arabien und den umliegenden Laendern.* [Preface by Dietmar Henze.] 3 vols. Kopenhagen, 1774-8; Hamburg, 1837 [Reprint Graz, 1968].

Olearius, Adam: *Moskowitische und Persische Reise: die Holsteinische Gesandtschaft beim Schah 1633 bis 1639.* Hrsg. v. Detlef Haberland. Stuttgart, 1986.
Olearius, ed. by Detlef Haberland

Olearius, Adam: *Vermehrte newe Beschreibung der muskowitischen und persischen Reyse [...].* Schleswig, 1656. Hrsg. v. Dieter Lohmeier. Tübingen, 1971. (Deutsche Neudrucke. Reihe Barock, Bd.21). *Olearius, ed. by Dieter Lohmeier*

Osterhammel, Jürgen: 'Reisen an die Grenzen der Alten Welt: Asien im Reisebericht des 17. und 18. Jahrhunderts.' In: Peter J. Brenner (ed.): *Der Reisebericht: die Entwicklung einer Gattung in der deutschen Literatur.* Frankfurt a.M., 1989. pp.224-60. (Suhrkamp taschenbuch 2097). *Osterhammel, Reisen*

Ostermeyer, Annemarie: 'Engelbert Kämpfers Hamelner Verwandte: Er wohnte als Schüler bei der Familie Prott in der Ritterstraße: Der Nachlaß des Japanreisenden.' In: *Feierabend an der Weser: Beilage der Deister- und Weserzeitung,* Nr.9 (6.3.1965), p.1.

Paulsen, Friedrich: *Geschichte des gelehrten Unterrichts auf den deutschen Schulen und Universitäten vom Ausgang des Mittelalters bis zur Gegenwart.* Bd.1. 3. Aufl. Berlin, Leipzig, 1919.

Pauly, Uli: *Sakoku: zu den Hintergründen von Japans Weg in die nationale Abschließung unter den Tokugawa.* Tokyo, 1989. (OAG aktuell, Nr.36).

Pochat, Götz: *Der Exotismus während des Mittelalters und der Renaissance: Voraussetzungen, Entwicklung und Wandel eines bildnerischen Vokabulars.* Stockholm, 1970. (Acta Universitatis Stockholmiensis, 21).

Puhstkuchen, Friedrich Christoph: *Beyträge zu den Denkwürdigkeiten der Grafschaft Lippe überhaupt und in Absicht auf die Religions- und Kirchen-Begebenheiten insonderheit.* Lemgo, 1769.

Red-hair medicine: Dutch-Japanese medical relations. Ed. by H. Beukers, A. M. Luyendijk-Elshout, M. E. van Opstall and F. Vos. Amsterdam, Atlanta/GA, 1991. (Nieuwe Nederlandse Bijdragen tot de Geschiedenis der Geneeskunde en der Natuurwetenschappen, No.36).

Rein, J[ohannes] J[ustus]: *Japan nach Reisen und Studien. Im Auftrage der Königlich Preußischen Regierung* dargestellt v. J.J.R. 2 vols. Leipzig, 1881-6.

Reinecke, Wilhelm: *Geschichte der Stadt Lüneburg.* Lüneburg, 1933 (Reprint 1977).

[Ritter, Carl:] *Die Erdkunde im Verhaeltnis zur Natur und zur Geschichte des Menschen, oder Allgemeine vergleichende Geographie, als sichere Grundlage des Studiums und Unterrichts in physicalischen und historischen Wissenschaften von Carl Ritter [...].* 19 vols. Berlin, 1817-59. *Ritter, Erdkunde*

Royle, Forbes J. & Frederick W. Headland: *A manual of materia medica and therapeutics including the preparation of the British Pharmacopoeia, and many other approved medicines.* 4th ed. London, 1865.

Sauerländer, Friedrich: 'Der Steinhof in Lieme und seine Besitzer.' In: *Lippische*

Mitteilungen aus Geschichte und Landeskunde, Bd.23 (1954), pp.138-58.

Scheibe, Siegfried: 'Zu einigen Grundprinzipien einer historisch-kritischen Ausgabe.' In: *Texte und Varianten [...]*. München, 1971. pp.1-44.

Schmeißer, Jörg: 'Zeichnungen und Drucke zu Engelbert Kaempfers *History of Japan/Geschichte und Beschreibung von Japan*.' In: *Engelbert Kaempfer: Werk und Wirkung [...]*. Stuttgart, 1992. pp.294-326.

[Schmitz, P. M. Edmond & Karl Meier-Lemgo:] 'Engelbert Kämpfer (1651-1716) und das persische Bitumen.' Von Karl Meier-Lemgo u. P. M. Schmitz. In: *Bitumen*, Jahrg.9 (1939), Hft.3-4, pp.49f., 76-9.

Schöne, Albrecht: *Kürbishütte und Königsberg: Modellversuch einer sozialgeschichtlichen Entzifferung poetische Texte*. Am Beispiel Simon Dach. München, 1975.

Schulz, H. von: 'Bibliographische Forschungen zur japanischen Kulturgeschichte im Japaninstitut zu Berlin.' In: *Japanisch-deutsche Zeitschrift zur Förderung der wissenschaftlich-technischen, politisch-wirtschaftlichen und kulturellen Beziehungen zwischen Japan und Deutschland*, N.F., Jahrg.1 (1928/29), Hft.2/3, pp.44-56; Hft.4, pp.78-84.

Schuster-Walser, Sibylla: *Das safawidische Persien im Spiegel europäischer Reiseberichte (1502-1722): Untersuchungen zur Wirtschafts- und Handelspolitik*. Baden-Baden, Hamburg, 1970.

Schutte Watt, Helga: *Deutsche Reisebeschreibungen von Kaempfer bis Stolberg: Vielfalt und Tradition des Genres im 18. Jahrhundert*. Diss. [Typescript.] Ann Arbor, 1978.

Schwanold, Heinrich: 'Engelbert Kämpfers Testament.' In: *Lippische Mitteilungen aus Geschichte und Landeskunde*, Bd.5 (1907), pp.41-61.

Siebold, Philipp Franz von: *Nippon: Archiv zur Beschreibung von Japan und dessen Neben- und Schutzländern Jezo mit den südlichen Kurilen, Sachalin, Korea und den Liukiu-Inseln*. Hrsg. v. seinen Söhnen. 2. Aufl. 2 vols. Würzburg, Leipzig, 1897.

[Solier, François:] *Histoire ecclesiastique des isles et royaumes du Iapon*. Recueillie par le P. François Solier, Religieux de la Compagnie de Iesus. Paris, 1628.

Spuler, Berthold: 'Fremde Augen: Überlegungen zu Engelbert Kämpfers Reisebeschreibung.' In: *Materialia turcica*, Bd.7/8 (1981/82), pp.325-35.

Starke, Fritz: *Lieme: Eine ländliche Siedlung in Gegenwart und Vergangenheit*. Lemgo, 1972.

Steenis, C. G. G. J. van (Hrsg.): *Flora Malesiana, being an illustrated systematic account of the Malaysian flora, including keys for determination, diagnostic descriptions, references to the literature, synonymy, and distribution, and notes on the ecology of its wild and commonly cultivated plants*. Haarlem, 1950. (Ser.I, vol.1).

Teleki, Paul: *Atlas zur Geschichte der Kartographie der japanischen Inseln. Nebst dem holländischen Journal der Reise Mathys Quasts und A. J. Tasmans zur Entdeckung der Goldinseln im Osten von Japan in dem Jahre 1639 und dessen deutscher Übersetzung*. Leipzig, 1909 (Reprint 1966).

Tell, Leander: 'Engelbert Kämpfer – en tysk läkare och upptäcktsresande i 1600-talets Orienten.' In: *Sydsvenska medicinhistoriska sällskapets årsskrift*, 1975, pp.124-42.   *Tell, Tysk läkare*

Tell, Leander: 'Svensk stormaktsdiplomat och orientexpert.' In: *Norrköpings Tidningar*, 1.6.1977, p.4.   *Tell, Stormaksdiplomat*

Terwiel, Barend J.: 'Kaempfer and Thai history: the documents behind the printed texts.' In: *Journal of the Royal Asiatic Society of Great Britain & Ireland*, 1989, no.1, pp.64-80. *Terwiel, Thai History*

Terwiel, Barend J.: 'Kaempfer's journal from Batavia and the writing of "Heutiges Japan".' In: *Engelbert Kaempfer: Werk und Wirkung [...]*. Stuttgart, 1992. pp.394-409. *Terwiel, Journal*

Terwiel, B[arend] J.: 'Unpublished sources: manuscript collections relating to Thai history in Europe.' In: *IIAS* [International Institute for Asien Studies, Leiden] *Newsletter*, no.3 (Autumn 1994), p.36. *Terwiel, Manuscript Collections*

Terwiel, Barend J. & Larry Sternstein: 'Prospects of Ayutthaya, capital of Siam 1690: a critical study of Engelbert Kaempfer's manuscripts.' In: *Engelbert Kaempfer: Werk und Wirkung [...]*. Stuttgart, 1992. pp.145-73.
Terwiel & Sternstein, Prospects

Texte und Varianten: Probleme ihrer Edition und Interpretation. Hrsg. v. Gunter Martens u. Hans Zeller. München, 1971.

Thommen, Eduard: 'Neues zur Schreibung des Namens Gingko.' *Verhandlungen der Naturforschenden Gesellschaft in Basel*, Bd.LX. (1949), pp.77-103.

Thunberg, Carl Peter: *Flora Iaponica, sistens plantas Insularum Iaponicarum [...]*. Leipzig, 1784.

Troebst, Stefan: 'Narva und der Außenhandel Persiens im 17. Jahrhundert: zum merkantilen Hintergrund schwedischer Großmachtpolitik.' In: *Studia baltica stockholmiensia*, vol.11 (Die schwedischen Ostseeprovinzen Estland und Livland im 16.-18. Jahrhundert), 1993, pp.161-78.

Valentini, Michael Bernhard: *Museum Museorum, oder Vollstaendige Schau-Buehne aller Materialien und Specereÿen [...] Aus andern Material Kunst- und Naturalien-Kammern / Oost- und West-Indischen Reisebeschreibungen [...]*. 2 vols. Frankfurt a.M., 1704-14.

Van de Velde, Paul: 'Die Achse, um die sich alles dreht. Imamura Gen'emon Eisei (1671-1736). Dolmetscher und ebenbürtiger "Diener" Kaempfers.' In: *Engelbert Kaempfer: Werk und Wirkung [...]*. Stuttgart, 1992. pp.174-93.

Varenius, Bernhard: *Descriptio regni Japoniae: Beschreibung des japanischen Reiches*. Unter Mitarbeit v. Lydia Brüll hrsg. v. Martin Schwind u. Horst Hammitzsch. Darmstadt, 1974.

Walravens, Hartmut: [Review of *Flora japonica*; see Sources.] In: *Sudhoffs Archiv für die Geschichte der Medizin und Naturwissenschaften*, Bd.69 (1985), Hft.1, p.104f.

Walter, Lutz (ed.): *Japan mit den Augen des Westens gesehen. Gedruckte europäische Landkarten vom frühen 16. bis zum 19. Jahrhundert*. München, 1994.

Weisgerber, G.: 'Muscat in 1688: Engelbert Kaempfer's report and engravings.' In: *The Journal of Oman Studies*, vol.5, 1979 (1982), pp.95-101.

Whittle, Tyler: *Pflanzenjäger: die abenteuerliche Suche nach dem grünen Gold*. [Includes: Joseph H. Biller: 'Über den deutschen Pflanzenjäger.'] München, 1971.

Widder, Felix: 'Die Rechtschreibung des Namens "Gingko".' In: *Phyton*, Jahrg.1 (1948), pp.47-52.

Wiesehöfer, Josef: 'Engelbert Kaempfer in Naqs-i Rustam und Persepolis.' In: Sancisi-Weerdenburg, Heleen & Jan Willem Drijvers (ed.): *Achaemenid history VII. Through travellers' eyes: European travellers on the Iranian monuments*. Proceedings of the 1989 Groningen Achaemenid History Workshop. Leiden, 1991. pp.71-87.

Winkler, Eberhard: *Die Leichenpredigt im deutschen Luthertum bis Spener.* München, 1967. (Forschungen zur Geschichte und Lehre des Protestantismus, Bd.XXXIV).

Würfel, Kurt: *Isfahan, das ist die 'British Library, Sloane 2923, fol.128r.'* Hälfte der Welt. Küsnacht, Zürich, 1974.

[Zedler, Johann Heinrich:] *Großes vollständiges Universal Lexikon aller Wissenschaften und Künste [...].* 64 vols., 4 suppl. vols. Halle, Leipzig, 1732-54.

Chronology

10.7.1610	Johannes Kemper is born in Wiedenbrück.
1644	Following studies in Rostock and Rinteln Kemper becomes pastor primarius of St Nicholas' Church in Lemgo.
ca.1644	Marriage to Christine Drepper.
30.4.1646	Their eldest son Joachim is born (†13.7.1706 in Lemgo).
16.9.1651	Engelbert, the second son of Johannes Kemper, is born in Lemgo.
ca.1654	After the death of Christine Drepper (ca.1654) his father marries Adelheid Pöppelmann (1637-1716).
15.7.1658	Birth of his brother Andreas (†25.8.1743 in Billertshausen). In the following years Johann (†27.1.1703 in Goldkronach), Johann Henrich (†2.4.1717 in Stavanger) and Johann Daniel (buried ca.29.12.1709 in Lemgo) are born.
from 1665	Attends the grammar school in Lemgo.
from 1667	Attends the grammar school in Hameln; journey to the Netherlands around this time.
from 1668	Attends the grammar school in Lüneburg.
20.12.1669	Birth of his sister Maria Magdalena.
from 1670	Attends the grammar school in Lübeck.
from 1672	Attends the grammar school in Danzig.
1.6.1673	Baptism of his sister Anna Catharina; another sister is baptised 11.2.1677, but dies as early as 11.3 the same year.
1673	Printing of the dissertation *Exercitatio politica de majestatis divisione in realem et personalem [...]* in Danzig.
8.6.1673-4.6.1674	Residence unrecorded, possibly in Torun.
1674-May 1676	Studies at the University of Cracow.
2.9.5-23.6.1676	Journey from Cracow via Warsaw, Torun and Danzig to Elbing.
24.6.1676-12.3.1677	Residence unrecorded, possibly already in Königsberg.
13.3.1677	Registration at the University of Königsberg.
August-October 1680	Journey to visit his father in Lemgo, where he was in September. Return to Königsberg via Verden, Bremen and Hamburg with his brother Andreas, who travels to Sweden.

149

August 1681	Journey to Sweden, where he studies at Uppsala and attends the court of Charles XI in Stockholm. Kaempfer is appointed secretary of the legation to the Persian court in Isfahan.
31.8.1682	His father dies in Lieme.
20.3.1683	The legation, led by Ludwig Fabritius, sets out via Åbo (Finland), Helsinki, Narva, Novgorod and Tver.
7.7-5.9.1683	Stay in Moscow, audience with Tsars Ivan and Peter.
5.9-1.11.1683	Journey from Moscow to Astrakhan.
12-22.11.1683	Crossing of the Caspian Sea, landing at Nisabad.
23.11.1683-29.3.1684	Rest at Nisabad and journey via Resht, Rudbar, Saveh, Qum and Kashan to Isfahan.
29.3.1684-20.11.1685	Sojourn in Isfahan, negotiations of the Swedes with Shah Suleyman. Kaempfer enters the service of the Dutch East India Company.
21.11.1685	Leaves Isfahan for Bandar Abbas.
3.12.1685	Visits the ruins at Naqsh-i Rustam and Persepolis.
4-8.12.1685	Stay in Shiraz and its surroundings.
29.12.1685-30.6.1688	Sojourn in Bandar Abbas on the Persian Gulf as physician at the Dutch factory.
June-August 1686	Medical leave at Bugun in the mountains north of Bandar Abbas.
1687	Observes the date harvest near Bandar Abbas. Writes the manuscript 'Palma arbor', the basis of the subsequent monograph on the date palm in the *Amoenitates exoticae*.
30.6.1688	Leaves for India via Muscat on the Horn of Arabia.
8.8.1688-autumn 1689	Voyages between the Malabar and Coromandel Coasts round Ceylon.
Autumn 1689-6.5.1690	Sojourn in Batavia (Java). Failure to obtain employment in the local hospital.
7.5-6.6.1690	Voyage to Japan, with a stay in Siam on the way.
6.6-11.7.1690	Visits the Dutch factory, ascends the Menam to Ayutthaya, visiting Bangkok on the way back.
11.7-24.9.1690	Continues the voyage to Japan in bad weather conditions.
21.9.1690-31.10.1692	Sojourn at Deshima
13.2-7.5.1691	First diplomatic mission to Edo (Tokyo) to pay homage to the Shogun, taking three to four weeks each way.
2.3-21.5.1692	Second diplomatic mission to Edo.
Autumn 1692	Return voyage to Java.

After 9.2.1693	Leaves Java with the homeward-bound Company fleet.
14.5.1693	Arrival at the Cape of Good Hope.
6.10.1693	Arrives in Amsterdam and stays with the Parvé family.
21.11.1693	Registration in the Medical Faculty of the National University in Leiden.
24.11.1693	Private oral examination in the Faculty of Medicine.
Beginning of 1694	Printing of the dissertation *Disputatio medica inauguralis exhibens decadem obsrvationum exoticarum [...]* by Abraham Elsevier in Leiden.
22.4.1694	Public examination (*rigorosum*).
April-July 1694	Stay in the Netherlands; visits his friends Mesdach in Leiden and Hovius in Rotterdam at the beginning of August.
1694	Returns to Lemgo and establishes himself as a physician.
5.10.1694	Buys the Steinhof in Lieme from his mother-in-law and siblings.
December 1698	Appointed physician in ordinary to Friedrich Adolf, Count of Lippe.
18.12.1700	Marries Maria Sophia Wilstach from Stolzenau an der Weser (1684-1761).
21.4.1702	Birth of their daughter Amalia Florentine at Stolzenau (buried 22.2.1705 in Lemgo).
3.7.1707	Baptism of a second daughter, Amalia (buried 23.12.1714 in Lemgo).
14.6.1710	Birth of a son, Friedrich Adolf, at Stolzenau an der Weser (buried 6.1.1715 in Lemgo).
1712	*Amoenitatum exoticarum politico-physico-medicarum fasciculi V [...]* published by the Meyersche Buchhandlung in Lemgo.
1716	*Phoenix persicus, seu Historia palmæ dactyliferæ* published in: Michael Bernhard Valentini, *Museum Museorum [...]*, Frankfurt am Main.
2.11.1716	Engelbert Kaempfer dies at 9 o'clock in the evening.
1723-1725	Sir Hans Sloane purchases Kaempfer's literary remains from his nephew Dr. Johann Hermann Kämpffer and Philip Zollman.
1727	Scheuchzer's translation of the work on Japan, *The History of Japan [...]*, is published in London in two volumes.
1729	The French translation of the work on Japan, *Histoire naturelle, civile, et ecclésiastique de l'empire du Japon [...]*

	published in The Hague; a Dutch translation follows in the same year.
1756	The first extract in German from the work on Japan, *Beschreibung des japanischen Reiches*, appears in part four of Du Halde's *Ausführliche Beschreibung des Chinesischen Reiches und der grossen Tartarey* (Rostock).
25.10.1773	Sale by auction of Kaempfer's library in Lemgo; the purchasers include Herder.
1773	First translation of the work on Japan into Russian.
1777-1779	Publication by Christian Wilhelm Dohm in Lemgo of the first complete, though revised, edition in German of the work on Japan under the title *Geschichte und Beschreibung von Japan*.
1791	Sir Joseph Banks publishes *Icones selectae plantarum quas in Japonia collegit et delineavit Engelbertus Kaempfer [...]*, a small selection of the botanical drawings made by Kaempfer in Japan.
1808	First selective translation of the work on Japan into Japanese.
1844-1847	The presumably first complete translation of the work on Japan into Japanese, title unknown; the manuscript was lost during the Meiji Restoration.
1867	Erection of the Kaempfer Memorial on the Hoher Wall in Lemgo.
1880	Still unpublished complete translation of the work on Japan into Japanese in 16 volumes.
1929	Karl Meier-Lemgo travels to London during his summer vacation and visits the British Museum to study the Kaempfer papers.
1937	Karl Meier-Lemgo's biography of Kaempfer, *Engelbert Kämpfer, der erste deutsche Forschungsreisende*, is published in Stuttgart.
1937-1939	Annual 'Kaempfer Festivals' in Lemgo.
1960	Second edition of Meier-Lemgo's biography of Kaempfer is published in Hamburg under the title *Engelbert Kämpfer (1651-1716) erforscht das seltsame Asien*.
1969	Karl Meier-Lemgo dies.
1971	The Engelbert-Kämpfer-Gesellschaft e.V. is founded in Lemgo.
1990	International Kaempfer symposia in Lemgo and Tokyo.

Index